AMAZING LOVE

AMAZING LOVE

BY

Corrie ten Boom

CHRISTIAN LITERATURE CRUSADE
Fort Washington, Pennsylvania 19034

CHRISTIAN LITERATURE CRUSADE

U.S.A.
Box 1449, Fort Washington, PA 19034

GREAT BRITAIN
51 The Dean, Alresford, Hants., SO24 9BJ

AUSTRALIA
P.O. Box 91, Pennant Hills, N.S.W. 2120

NEW ZEALAND
P.O. Box 10-192, Balmoral, Auckland 4

Copyright© 1953
Christian Literature Crusade
London

First Edition 1953
First American Edition 1971

ISBN 0-87508-018-9

PRINTED IN THE UNITED STATES OF AMERICA

FOREWORD

"YE shall be witnesses unto Me", said Jesus to His disciples, "unto the uttermost part of the earth." Corrie ten Boom is one of that number. Having found for herself the victory that overcomes the world in the horrors of a concentration camp, she cannot keep her secret to herself. She has become a world-wide witness, a troubadour of Christ. She shares with us in these pages, with all the vividness of first-hand experience, contacts and conversations with all sorts in camps and jails, with actresses and students, with sophisticated and illiterate: and I lay down this manuscript saying, like those two disciples of old, "Did not our heart burn within us, while He talked with us by the way?" For I met, not Corrie, but Corrie's Christ. I was blessed again and again by the instances of her own child-like dependence on Him as her wisdom, by His responses to her faith, and by the wise and winning ways in which she has been able to commend Him to so many. May many who read these living chapters see Him again, in the simplicity of faith, as our all-sufficiency, and be stirred, as I have been, to a bolder faith.

NORMAN P. GRUBB

CONTENTS

PLANS

Human hearts are amazingly alike.

THE silence of night had fallen on seven hundred women, lying tightly packed together, asleep in the barracks of a concentration camp.

Bep, my sister, awakened me and repeated to me in a whisper what God had told her about the work that would be waiting for us after our release.

" We must open a home for people who have suffered so much here and in other places where life has been completely disrupted by war. But the most important part of our task will be to tell everyone who will listen that Jesus is the only answer to the problems that are disturbing the hearts of men and of nations. We shall have the right to speak because we can tell from our experience that His light is more powerful than the deepest darkness. Surely, nothing could be darker than our experiences here. I keep telling myself, ' things cannot possibly grow worse ', but every day we see that misery only deepens. How wonderful that the reality of His presence is greater than the reality of the hell about us! We shall have to do a lot of travelling, but we must never spend our energies in collecting funds. God will provide everything we need: money, health, wisdom, and the necessary languages. All of our efforts must go into bringing the Gospel, for we shall have many opportunities."

Bep's eyes did not see the dirty throng around us. She was gazing into the future, and a glow of happiness brightened her emaciated face.

Three days later she passed away, and ten days later, just one week before all women of my age were killed, I was released from the concentration camp.

In this book I shall describe some of my experiences during the first years of my wanderings. Why should I do this? Because I have discovered that there are many people who need this message.

Human hearts are amazingly alike. As I talk with people in America, England, Switzerland, Germany, and Holland, I frequently find the same need, the same ignorance of what we can be in Jesus Christ, if only we accept the Bible in a simple, childlike way as the Word of God, the Word that teaches us the foolishness of God that is wiser than the wisdom of men, the love of God that passes all understanding.

When we read the Bible we should never use as our guide the wisdom of men or the standards of our own reason.

I was once a passenger aboard a ship that was being guided by radar. The fog was so dense we couldn't see even the water about us. But the radar screen showed a streak of light, indicating the presence of another ship far ahead. The radar penetrated the fog and picked up its image. So, also, is faith the radar that sees reality through the clouds.

The reality of the victory of Christ can be seen only by faith, which is our radar. Our faith perceives what is actual and real; our senses perceive only that which is limited to three dimensions and comprehended by our intellect. Faith sees more.

I am not a scholar, but much of the little I do know, I learned as I faced death in front of the crematorium in Ravensbruck. That is why God sometimes uses me to help people who know far more than I.

FORGIVENESS

" And when ye stand praying, forgive, if ye have ought against any: that your Father also which is in heaven may forgive you your trespasses."—Mark 11: 25.

Why should we hold on to the sins of others while our own sins have been cast into the depths of the sea ?

I WAS a guest on one of the farms on the vast prairies of Kansas. How far the horizons stretch out on every hand! And how clear the air! We Hollanders are accustomed to a shading of colour and line in our landscape, due to the atmosphere. But here everything is clearly visible at three hundred yards or more, and seems close by. When the sun sets the shadows fall stark and clear from barn, cows, and even the tassled corn.

The family with which I was staying was a large one, and I always have an especially good time when I am taken right into the life of a typical American family. The youngest daughter here was just finishing high school, and all of us planned to attend the graduation exercises the following week.

All of us? Something was threatening to mar the joy of that happy occasion. For months past there had been dissension between the father and his eldest son. In a fit of anger the father had shown his son the door and forbidden him ever to cross its threshold again.

The mother told me the whole story in confidence. For her the graduation festivities would be no joy. "My boy has a farm not far from here," said she, "but I'm sure he will not want to come."

We prayed together about it, and then I waited for the opportunity I knew God would prepare for me.

I was having quite a few interesting experiences on the farm. I had helped drive the tractor, and, although the farmer stood behind me, I was still proud of having finished the corners so neatly.

One afternoon I went riding. The whole family stood watching as I mounted. The horse was being difficult, and, ignoring the reins entirely, walked over to the watering-trough, began to drink, and then put his feet into the trough. I had all I could do to keep from pitching forward over his head. Finally, with the efforts of all, the horse was led to the road; but I had to take a lot of bantering advice and laughter about my first riding-lesson. Once on the road, however, everything was fine. The horse was walking quietly now. The whole prairie lay stretched out before me, I inhaled deeply the pure air. The corn rustled and the wind played with my hair.

What a delight it is to look out over the world from the back of a horse!

Then the farmer rode up alongside of me, and before I knew it, there it was, the opportunity for which we had prayed.

"Have you ever prayed 'forgive us our debts as we forgive our debtors'?" I asked him. "Do you know what has become of your sins? If you believe in Jesus Christ and belong to Him, they have been cast into the depths of the sea, and that's very deep. But then He expects also that you will forgive the sins of your boy and cast them into the depths of the sea. Just imagine how you would feel if there should be another war, if your son had to go back into service and was killed in action. Don't you think you should forgive him right now? The love which God has for you in Christ Jesus is the same love that He will pour out into your heart through His spirit. If you open your heart to receive it, then His love will become your love, and His forgiveness your forgiveness."

All through the conversation I continued praying that the demon of bitterness would not win the conflict going on in the heart of the farmer.

After we had been riding for some time in silence, he said suddenly, " I'm going to see my son tonight. Will you go with me?"

And so we did. The old man was a bit uncomfortable as he stepped into the house. The son looked up in surprise. Then the father put his hand on the shoulder of the young man and said—was I hearing correctly?—" My boy, will you forgive me?"

I turned and walked quickly around to the other side of the house, but I could still hear the son's reply, " But, Father, I should ask you for forgiveness."

The graduation party was a great success.

THE WAY BACK

Yesterday is a cancelled cheque.
Today is cash.
Tomorrow is a promissory note to them that accept the victory of Jesus.

YEARS ago when my father was assisting in the rehabilitation of prisoners he asked me if I would like to help him and become a regular visitor to prison cells. I answered, "Please, Father, don't ask me to do anything like that. I wouldn't dare enter even a prison, to say nothing of going into the cells." But now that I myself have been a prisoner this fear is completely gone, and I try whenever possible to preach the Gospel in prisons.

I had received an invitation to visit Sing Sing, and was now about to see this modern penal institution.

In the parking-lot were the cars of a visiting football team that had come to match its skill with the Sing Sing eleven. Several gates were opened and closed behind us, and then we were driven in a real prison-van up the high hill on top of which the buildings are located. I couldn't help thinking of the van in which I had been taken to the prison at Scheveningen. Other than this, however, there was no similarity, for this did not look much like a prison.

On an open space in front of the chapel were many

13

prisoners walking about freely, and here they did not
wear uniform.   The view over the river was beautiful.

In the chapel there were about a hundred prisoners
and only one guard. It looked like an ordinary church
service.   The men sang with enthusiasm, and one after
another suggested a hymn.   (Several of the prisoners
were taking a correspondence course in Bible study at
Moody Bible Institute.)   There was an " openness "
that made it easy for me to speak.   My text was " For
we wrestle not against flesh and blood, but against
principalities . . . against spiritual wickedness in high
places " (Eph. 6:12).

I told the men how, in Ravensbruck where I so often
saw death about me, I had suddenly realized that life is,
after all, very simple, but that it is we who make it in-
volved.   The devil is more powerful than we are, but
Jesus is more powerful than the devil.   Now if we
belong to Jesus, we are on the victorious side.   He
came to destroy the works of the devil.   We are not
only striving towards victory but fighting from the
position of victory.

After the service several of the prisoners came to
shake hands with me.   With one of them, a coloured
man, I had a long talk, and finally he said, " For a long
time I have been unable to find the way back.   Now
I know—Jesus is the way."

AN UNEXPECTED FEAST

On Calvary two malefactors were crucified : which of them is you?

IN the smaller towns and villages of the United States the sheriff's house often serves also as a jail. It was on a Sunday afternoon that we rang the bell of such a home and asked if I could speak to the prisoners.

"Go right ahead," said the sheriff. "We haven't many customers right now, but if you think it worth-while I'll be glad to take you to them."

It was a wretched little jail. Along one side of the cells were barred doors standing open. A narrow passage in front of the cells was also barred, and beyond these bars were some small windows. There were only three prisoners, a man and two boys.

Right here I had one of those rare spiritual feasts that can come to one so unexpectedly in life. In the narrow passage in front of the cells I sat down and began to talk, my Bible open on my knees. The man was sitting on a stool at a small table. One of the boys sat on the floor with his legs crossed and his back against the bars. The other boy stood leaning against the door of his dirty cell.

After I had told them about the victory of Christ over sin the man began to speak. He told his story

15

of drunkenness and crime, and then turned to the boy beside him.

"What she said is true. It's only since coming here to serve my term that I've done what she advises. I've said ' Yes ' to Jesus. And it isn't hard as I thought it would be. You know what she said about faith being like that radar apparatus through which you could see a ship coming right through the fog? That's exactly the way it is. I have always seen only the clouds and fog, and have never understood that the ship might be there. Now, suddenly, I see Him, right through everything. Jesus is a reality. He loves you so much that if you were the only human being on earth He would still have thought it worthwhile to die for you on the Cross."

"I've never had a single person who cared anything about me," said the boy.

"Then you've found your Man now. For God so loved the world that He gave His only begotten Son, that whosoever—and that means you, too—believeth on Him should not perish, but have everlasting life."

That afternoon both boys surrendered their lives to Christ.

BE NOT AFRAID

Do not ask " what can I do ? " but " what can He not do ? "

THINGS do not always work out as smoothly as they did in the home of the sheriff.

One day I was permitted to join a " team " that worked regularly in a large prison. It was a most unusual building. We set our portable organ down in a long narrow corridor barred at both ends. Only three faces were visible behind the barred cells both to the right and left of us. Evidently I would have to keep turning my head from one direction to the other while speaking.

One of the women opened the service by singing to the accompaniment of the organ. She sang in a very affected manner, and the response was anything but favourable. At both ends of the corridor the prisoners began shrieking, yelling, and screaming to drown the voice of the singer. But she went calmly on with her song. Mixed with it all I could hear scornful, jeering laughter. Then one of the young men with us began to pray, speaking in a very unctuous manner. The effect was even worse. The prisoners had found a pail and were rolling it back and forth over the floor. The din was terrific. " Lord, must I speak in this place? I cannot," I prayed in desperation.

" Be not afraid; only believe. You can do all things

through Him who strengthens you. There will be a great victory," said the Lord to me.

Then I dared to start. The noise grew even worse. Benches were thrown to the floor. There was an infernal clamour from all sides. But I was no longer afraid. I had the promise of victory, and so I tried to shout above the din. I bellowed, "When I was alone in a cell for four months——"

Suddenly there was a dead silence. What? That lady alone in a cell for four months? Prisoners always feel very sorry for me when I tell them about this part of my life. To be in solitary confinement is a severe punishment everywhere in the world. Most prisoners have learned that from experience.

Above the heads of the three prisoners behind the bars appeared more faces. They brought benches and chairs and climbed up on them to see us better. More and more faces appeared at both ends of the corridor. It was deadly quiet now, and I talked and talked, for three quarters of an hour. There was joy in my heart. The love of God was there. God's Spirit was working, and when I had finished, and the minister who was with us asked the men to surrender their lives to Christ, there were six who said " Yes ". The minister went to one end of the corridor and I to the other, each taking three of these men who had raised their hands, to speak to them further. Now I could see that there was a large room beyond the end of the corridor where many prisoners were gathered together. Evidently all the men had to listen to the service whether they wanted to hear the Word or not.

It was quiet as I spoke to the three men. Then I looked around and addressed them all.

"Never before have I heard such awful noise during a service as here when I first began to speak. I was so glad that you soon quieted down. But do you know what I'm a bit afraid of now? That you will tease these men who held up their hands, or laugh at them. Please don't do that. These three men have made their decision for Jesus Christ, and are now standing on the side of victory. They have received a booklet called 'The Gospel According to St. John'. Let them read it to you now and then. I hope that some day you, too, will say 'Yes' to Christ. I know that it will make you happy."

THE WORD OF GOD IS LIVING
AND POWERFUL

" The sword of the Spirit which is the Word of God " is far more powerful than our own arguments.

WE were sitting on the veranda of a university dormitory, and a Mrs. Jameson was commenting on the lecture I had given only a few moments before.

" What you just told the students was very interesting, but I do not think you are right. Please do not take it ill of me, but I have had a wider experience than you. I am a member of an association that has taken me all over the world, and I have talked with outstanding persons in India, Arabia, Japan, and many other countries. I have discussed the road of life through time and eternity with Mohammedans, Brahmins, Shintoists, and many others. There were excellent people among them who came to know God without Jesus Christ. You told the students so positively that we need Him, but that is not true."

" Your argument is not with me, but with the Bible," said I. " It is not I who say so, but the Bible. Jesus said, ' No man cometh unto the Father but by Me ' " (John 14:6).

I felt somewhat abashed. A sense of inadequacy often comes over me when I talk with people who are so much better informed than I. At such times this work seems much to difficult for me. Later on I talked it over with a friend who said, " You should not try to be anything but an open channel for the Spirit of God. You never can be anything else, even though you may think so at times. Follow the pathway of obedience, and you will be used by God far beyond your own powers."

A reception was being held in Ottawa, Canada, for all who wished to meet H.R.H. Prince Bernhard of the Netherlands. It was a pleasure to see so many Hollanders together. The Prince looked tired, but was cheerful and kind to everyone who addressed him. Photographers surrounded him as they took pictures of him from all sides, in conversation with some important person, or with a sweet country child in his arms.

I met many old acquaintances. And then, suddenly, I was face to face with Mrs. Jameson.

" I am glad to see you," said she. " You know, I just cannot forget what you said to me when you spoke at our university. Jesus said, ' No man cometh unto the Father but by Me ' ; I keep thinking about that."

" How wonderful! " I said. " You have listened to the voice of God. Now go on listening and read the Bible. He still has much more to say to you."

The Word of God is living and powerful.

THE SEA IS DEEP

I know beyond the shadow of doubt
My debt of sin has been wiped out.

THERE was to be a dinner party in a beautiful home beside a river. Several students had also been invited. It was approximately a two-hour drive from the city, but the people of Georgia do not seem to consider that a great distance. My host and I drove out along roads bright with oleanders blooming on either side.

We arrived just in time to see a glorious sunset. The sky above the water was ablaze with blue and gold as we sat on the beautiful terrace among the palms and enjoyed the warm evening air.

Coloured servants were moving quietly about serving refreshments. It seemed as if time itself moved more slowly here. No one was in a hurry, nor was the conversation superficial.

I had spoken the night before on the subject, " The problem of sin has been solved on the Cross of Jesus Christ ". And I was glad to see that Jack was present tonight, because I had seen a look of obvious distaste on his face during my talk the night before and had not had the opportunity of discussing it with him.

This is an example of my reason for feeling that there is a great disadvantage in not speaking more than once to the same group. The danger is that the work then becomes superficial. The friendly and even sincere words, " I enjoyed your message ", are not the only result I want to attain. I want people to come to an understanding of who Jesus is and how He wants to be the renewer of our lives.

And now Jack said, " I believe that there is remission of sins through Jesus Christ, but redemption? No, I can't see that. You said yesterday, ' The blood of Jesus Christ cleanseth us from all sin.' You showed us your hand and illustrated the text by saying, ' This morning my hand was dirty. Where is the dirt now? I don't know, I washed my hands. And so, too, Jesus washes away our sins. He casts them into the depths of the sea. They are gone, as far as the East is removed from the West.' That may be your opinion, but I don't believe it. We have to carry the consequences of our sins as long as we live. I believe in the forgiveness of sins, yes, but not in redemption."

After dinner we continued our talk in the garden. There were only three of us now; John, with whom I had been working for the past two weeks, and Jack, who was relating his experiences to us. It can be such a release to unburden one's soul completely.

It was a sad story.

" We were not very good boys in high school. I dated a lot of different girls, and one time things went wrong. I had to marry the girl; and four months later the baby came. Nobody knows that I am married, and no one must find it out. I want to become a minister; but if people hear about this my whole career will be gone. I am living a lie, and don't know what to do about it. I'll have to bear the consequences of my sin as long as I live. And that is what I mean by ' forgiveness, yes; but no remission '."

As he spoke I continued praying for wisdom. How could I explain to him the mystery of the renewal of life through the victory of Jesus Christ?

Then John began to speak.

" Nevertheless, there is redemption. Jesus does not patch things up. He renews. If you will ask Him to go back with you to that dark spot in your life, He will change its darkness into light. That was His purpose in coming to us. He delivered us from all sin.

" Jesus lifts you up out of the cycle of cause and effects into the realm of His wonderful love. And one of the products of that love is grace."

" What is grace?"

" It's what Isaiah meant when he said: ' Instead of the thorn shall come up the fir tree.' Instead of a curse there will be a blessing.

" ' Instead of the brier shall come up the myrtle tree.' Instead of a sinner there will be a saint.

" In Christ we are, you and I, the righteousness of God. Don't you understand that?

" Of course you don't. We'll understand these things only when we get to heaven and have new minds, and other means of perception. But even now we can understand these things by faith. If you will now accept in faith that Jesus is the victor over the past, present, and future of everyone who surrenders his life completely to Him, He will change that dark spot in your life into a blessing. Then you will always see in that woman and child a living symbol of the forgiveness and redemption of Jesus Christ."

"But what must I do?" asked Jack. "I have been converted, as people call it, and I have accepted Jesus as my personal Saviour."

"You still have to surrender your life completely to Him. Turn over all the keys of your life to Him. To lose your life for His sake means to save it. In His great love He demands your complete surrender."

Jack looked around. We were alone in the garden. From the house came a hubbub of many voices.

"I am willing to do it, but I don't know how to express it," said he.

"Just ask the Spirit of God to give you the right words."

All three of us then prayed, and Jack said, "I don't understand these things, but here I am, Lord, I know that You have said ' Him that cometh unto Me I will in no wise cast out ', and ' A broken and a contrite heart, O God, Thou wilt not despise '."

Just then I was called into the house, for they expected me to speak again to the guests. An hour later as I was leaving, Jack said to me, "Corrie, I can laugh again; I haven't been able to laugh for a year. But now I am free."

And I knew that it was true.

I don't know what the results of his deliverance will be, but he will no longer have to live a lie. His life is in good hands.

"If the Son therefore shall make you free, ye shall be free indeed" (John 8: 36). And Jack will be used to help many who are in despair because of the consequences of their sins.

Our sins in the depths of the sea!

How tremendously great is the remission and redemption of sins through Jesus Christ!

Many Christians do not sufficiently realize the work which Jesus Christ is doing for us at this very moment. Many of us believe that He died for our sins. We believe in His death and resurrection, but we forget that after His resurrection, He ascended into heaven and sat down on the right hand of the Father and began to live for us as truly as He died for us.

The devil makes accusations against us day and night. But Jesus is our Advocate. In Him we are the righteousness of God (II Cor. 5:21).

If, after having been forgiven for a sin, we are still worrying about it, even for five minutes more, we are robbing both Him and ourselves of much joy.

" Resist the devil, and he will flee from you " (Jas. 4:7). No better weapon could be found to use against him than this text.

The consciousness of sin may degenerate into defeatism, " It's too bad, but that's the way I am." The devil rejoices when we are defeated, but is afraid of the consciousness of victory.

The devil makes us conscious of sin.

The spirit of God makes us conscious of sin, and then conscious of victory.

NEVER AGAIN TO GERMANY

When Jesus tells us to love our enemies, He Himself will give us the love with which to do it. We are neither factories nor reservoirs of His love, only channels. When we understand that, all excuse for pride is eliminated.

RETURNING to Holland after my release from the German concentration camp at Ravensbruck, I said, "One thing I hope is that I'll never have to go to Germany again. I am willing to go wherever God may want me to go; but I hope He'll never send me to Germany."

If we want to experience the guidance of God in our lives, we must accept one condition: obedience to Him.

On my trips to the United States I often spoke on the conditions in Europe during the post-war years, and when I talked of the chaos in Germany, people sometimes asked me "Why don't you go to Germany, since you know the language?"

But I didn't want to go.

Then darkness came into my fellowship with God; when I asked for His guidance, there was no answer.

Now God does not want us ever to be in doubt as to what His guidance is, and so I knew that something had come between God and me, and I prayed, "Lord is there some disobedience in my life?"

The answer was very distinct: "Germany."

Before me I could see again the land I had left in
1944. In my mind I could hear the harsh voices,
" Schneller, aber schneller (faster, faster) "; and my
answer to God was long in coming.

" Yes, Lord, I'll go to Germany, too. I'll follow
wherever you lead."

Then, when I returned to Holland from the United
States, I learned that it was not yet possible for Hollanders to obtain a visa for visiting Germany.

And I was glad.

I received an invitation to attend an International
Conference in Switzerland; and God told me that I
would meet some Germans there who would help me
obtain a visa. Arriving at the conference, I found
representatives from many countries, but not one single
German.

And I was glad.

But on the last day of the conference, there were two
new arrivals. The instant they appeared, I could see
they were Germans. I asked them if they could help
me with my papers, and one of the late-comers turned
out to be a director of the " Evangelisches Hilfswerk ",
the church organization for the assistance of refugees.

" If I send you an invitation to come to Germany,
you will be able to get your visa," said he.

And so I went back to Germany.

Was it difficult? At times it was, at times it was not.

There is a sanctified Germany, and a poisoned Germany. There is a Germany that has lost everything,
where the hearts of people are a vacuum. Who is going to fill them? It is wonderful to be able to speak

there about Him who renews hearts, and fills them with His joy.

Years ago I told the story of Jesus' feeding the five thousand with five loaves and two fishes to a class of feeble-minded boys. Carl had become so absorbed in the story that he jumped to his feet and shouted, "There is enough, there is enough, take as much as you want, there is enough!"

Dear little Carl, I wish more people were as much on fire about it as you.

Here we have the great riches of the Bible, and people misuse their time quibbling about its interpretation.

Is this a time for controversy?

Just imagine that your house was on fire, and the firemen were wrangling about their uniforms.

I heard that General MacArthur asked for a thousand missionaries to preach the Gospel in Japan. There is a hunger for the Gospel in that country. The harvest is plenteous; the labourers are few.

Not only there.

Also in Germany.

MY CHOCOLATE SERMON

Though Jesus in Bethlehem a thousand times were born, and not in my heart, I would still be forlorn.

I WAS again in a German concentration camp for women.

Wooden barracks in the heart of a beautiful forest.

The superintendent was a friendly German woman who tried to keep her charges under control in " the democratic manner ": no jumping to attention, no bellowed commands, no interminable roll calls as in Ravensbruck. But still it was a concentration camp, and it was surrounded by a barbed-wire fence.

In the camp I encountered " Aufseherinnen ", women guards from Ravensbruck, where I myself had been imprisoned. Now they were prisoners, and I was free, free to walk out of that gate any time to the freedom of the life outside. They would have to stay. I had come here to show these people the way to real freedom. I had come to speak of the love of God that passes all understanding, to tell about Jesus Christ, who came into this world to make people happy under all circumstances.

But—it was not easy to reach through to these people.

In one of the factory barracks they were sitting in

front of me. Each one had brought a chair from her own dormitory barracks. Their faces were glum, and it seemed as if I were addressing a stone wall. I kept praying that the love of God would fill me, and shine through me. But all I could see was aversion and bitterness.

All of the women had Bibles with them, and were evidently very familiar with them, because they found the texts I cited without any difficulty.

After having spoken in this camp twice, I consulted the superintendent.

" Can you tell me why I get no response at all?"

She laughed and answered, " The women have said to me, ' This Dutch woman speaks in such a simple way. We Germans are more highly cultivated, and so much more profound in our theology.' I'm afraid you won't get along too well together. But why don't you try once more. You have permission to speak three times."

When I got home, I went down on my knees.

" Lord, won't you please give me a message?" I prayed. " I am not cultured enough, and not profound enough theologically for these ' National-socialistic ' women." And then came the answer:

" Chocolate."

It made no sense to me. Would you call that a message? But suddenly I caught on. I had in my possession a box of chocolate, something that was not on the market anywhere in Germany, to say nothing of in a concentration camp.

The next day I set out for camp full of new courage.

There they were, sitting once more in front of me, resistance and distaste on every sombre face.

But I said, "This is my last visit with you, and so I brought you a little treat—some chocolate."

How those faces lighted up! What a luxury a piece of chocolate was to those poor prisoners! All at once we were friends. Some of them even asked me to write my name and address in their Bibles.

When I began to speak, I said, "No one has said anything to me about the chocolate."

"Oh, yes, we did; we thanked you."

"Yes, of course, but no one questioned me about this chocolate. No one asked whether it had been manufactured in Holland or what quantities it contained of cocoa, sugar, milk, or vitamins. You have done exactly what I intended you to do: you have eaten and enjoyed it."

Then I took up my Bible and said, "It is just the same with this Book. If I read about the Bible in a scientifically theological or scholarly way it does not make me happy. But if I read in it that God so loved the world that He gave His only begotten Son, that whosoever (and that means Corrie ten Boom also) believeth in Him should not perish but have everlasting life, then I am really happy. When I read in this Book that there are many mansions in my Father's house, I know that He is also preparing a place for me."

God's Spirit was working. Barriers fell away, and understanding and longing were born in the eyes before me, a hunger to hear more of that love that passes all understanding.

Many months later I was in a larg. hospital. An emaciated patient seemed to recognize me.

"Don't you remember me?" she asked.

I had to admit, much to my regret, that I couldn't place her.

"Last year I was a prisoner in Darmstadt," she said. "When you visited the camp, you preached on chocolate. That was the moment of my conversion. Since then I have not read *about* the Bible but *in* it. Now I have to die, but I am not afraid. I, too, have read in His Book that in my Father's house are many mansions. And this I know: Jesus is preparing one also for me."

PREACHING THE GOSPEL IN
WORD AND DEED

The devil often laughs when we work, but he trembles when we pray.

AN invitation came to work in Darmstadt for one week. I was very happy to accept it, but asked if it would be possible to enlist the aid of a prayer circle there. Upon my arrival, I found a group of twenty-six people gathered together from the different churches of Darmstadt. I didn't know whether it was their first meeting as a prayer group, but I found them loyal helpers. Every day a number of the group would meet with me to pray about the work that had been done on the past day, and for the work of the next one. Wherever there is such prevailing prayer something is bound to happen, and there was great blessing during that week.

After my departure the group continued to meet in weekly prayer sessions. It strikes me that here is an excellent prayer discipline. The meetings are opened and closed by reading the Word of God. Everyone present prays briefly and clearly. At times they listen in silence to what God may have to say to them, for, most important of all, is the fact that God speaks through His Spirit.

Where men are praying, God will be working.

Returning to Darmstadt a year later, I found the prayer circle still larger. There must have been at least forty in the group.

My first request was for permission to work again in the same concentration camp where I had preached the Gospel the year before. But I heard that the camp was empty. Most of the women had been released, and the worst cases transferred to prison.

The refugee problem in Germany, serious as it is to-day, was tremendous during the first years after the close of war. There were said to be nine million people without adequate shelter. There were the " Umsiedler " from the Russian zone and from other countries behind the " Iron Curtain " such as Czechoslovakia, Poland, and Hungary, and then the countless numbers who had been bombed out of their homes.

For a small amount of money we rented the unused camp, and with united efforts made the barracks as habitable as possible. Soon the refugees poured in.

Some of the faithful members of the prayer group took a very active part in the work; I myself travelled on, but promised to return as soon as possible.

Now here I was, back again. The gate was un-guarded. The barbed-wire fences were camouflaged by shrubs, or here and there removed entirely.

I walked through the barracks. The work was still in its early stages, and separate rooms had not yet been built. Several families were living together. One of the barracks was locked, and we found that the men who lived there had taken the key away with them that morning. That aroused a bit of suspicion in us; but, even so, we were not prepared for the horrible disorder we found after securing another key to open the door. The beds were unmade, the floor littered with fuel; rubbish was piled high in the corner.

Was it possible that human beings lived here?

"We'll certainly tell these men tonight what we think of them," said the superintendent. But I exclaimed quickly, "Oh, no, please don't scold them. These people have wandered from country to country and from one camp to another, and they have forgotten how to live in a house with love and consideration for it. We must help them. Let's tell them we're going to have a party next Wednesday, and that we expect them to have everything clean and tidy."

The prayer group was enthusiastic about the idea. Everyone had a share in the preparations for the party; and when Wednesday arrived there was a transformation in the main barracks. The tables were covered with white cloths, and there were flowers, flowers everywhere, for it was Springtime.

Three women and five children had arrived in camp that very day, and added to our company. There were refreshments, coffee and cake, white bread and fruit. We sang roundelays which sounded fine. All of the members of the prayer group were present; and they helped the men, who were at first ill at ease, to feel at home. So there was a pleasant and happy atmosphere, and everyone listened attentively as I spoke to them. I honestly cannot remember ever having attended a more enjoyable party.

During the course of the evening, a thin, shabbily dressed man stood up and clicked against his teacup.

" Friends," he said, " I have been wandering about for nine years.   Tonight I feel like a human being for the first time in many years."

We received excellent co-operation in this work from the municipal government and from the " Evangelisches Hilfswerk ".   In their spare time the men were permitted to build themselves houses in a forest near by. After some time there were to be two villages, one for five hundred, and another for three hundred families. As soon as one family left, other refugees would take its place.

The work grew.   A Sunday school was organized for the children, a Bible study group for the women; and every Sunday there were worship services.   But the men wanted to spend every spare minute in building their homes, and weren't much interested in taking part in the services.   Then an original plan was worked out.

There were four neighbouring ministers and churches co-operating in conducting the worship services.   Each minister and his parishioners, therefore, had a turn once in four weeks.   Now, in order to persuade the men to come to church, the ministers and their parishioners decided that the same week in which they conducted the service they would also spend one afternoon building houses.

The Gospel in word and deed.

ONCE A SOLDIER OF HITLER

"I am come a light into the world, that whosoever believeth on me should not abide in darkness."—John 12:46.

GERMANY can be very depressing, not only because of the ruins of its houses, but even more because of its many ruined lives.

A young man and I were walking in a pleasant valley between green hills. The weather was lovely; it was a Spring day, full of promise. Birds were singing, the skies were blue, and fresh green blossomed on trees and shrubs. Every year, since the Spring season I spent in a prison cell, I have been doubly thankful for freedom whenever there is a beautiful Spring day.

The face of the young man beside me did not look happy. I wanted so much to share my joy with him, to open his eyes to the beauties of nature around him, so I prayed, "Lord, show me the way; help me to understand him. Let your love shine through me."

Then he began to speak. He told me about his youth. At the age of fourteen he had been enrolled in one of Hitler's schools. It was a fine school, and the boys had everything their hearts could desire. "When I was fourteen," he said, "I had my own canoe, at sixteen, my own horse, and at eighteen, my own car. I was nineteen when I became a Storm Trooper, and was put in charge of a camp where Storm

Troopers were punished for minor offences. I approved heartily of the rigid discipline maintained there. That was the way to develop a strong and tough generation. I have been reared systematically in hardness and cruelty. There is only one ideal, and that is power. Everything you spoke of in your talks was weak. You spoke of forgiveness. Forgiveness is weakness."

" Can you imagine, Karl Heinz, that forgiveness requires more strength than hatred?"

" O, no: hatred is strong, and forgiveness is weak. Once, when I was seventeen years old, I saw a ship with thousands of prisoners aboard. It was sunk before my eyes, and it did not move me at all. I am well trained."

The loveliness of the Spring day was gone. I saw no blossoms, no fresh green buds, only a bird pulling a worm out of the ground. The worm writhed in its beak. It was not the only worm that was being bitten to death.

The young man beside me was not the only German boy who had been poisoned.

Poor world!

I was suddenly dead tired.

" Let us sit down here for a few minutes, Karl Heinz."

A beautiful panorama stretched out before us. We were sitting on the top of a hill, and could see far into the distance.

The day will come when the righteousness of God shall cover the earth as the waters cover the sea.

In my imagination I could see again the concentration camp. Thousands of prisoners were streaming toward me, and I struggled to go against the tide. Bep was beside me. What ugly, bitter, and depraved faces we were seeing! I longed to escape the disharmony.

Then Bep said, " I am beginning to love the multitude."

I prayed, " Lord Jesus, come quickly and fulfil your promise to make all things new. Grant that I, and all your followers, may redeem the time, for the days are so evil. Save this young man beside me. Fill me with your love so that it will flow through me and touch him."

When I got back to the place of our conference, Werner said to me, " I saw you leave with Karl Heinz, and we have been holding a prayer meeting for you. Were you able to help him?"

" I don't know, Werner; I prayed continually, ' Lord, make me an open channel for your love '. But look, why don't you have another talk with him?"

" I'll be glad to do that. I understand Karl Heinz perhaps better than you do. I myself was once a soldier of Hitler. Now I am a soldier of Jesus Christ!"

HOLLAND

"We are the children of a King and have in our possession the key to our Father's storehouse. All its treasures are ours to use at any moment."—Eva von Thiele Winkler.

I WAS back in Holland. How wonderful it is to be in one's own country! I love Holland. Nowhere else do you see such colours. Look at that field of grass! It is a different shade of green from the next field, and the one beyond it is still another shade. The moist atmosphere of Holland transforms the country-side into a symphony of tints and shades.

We were sitting on a dyke looking far out over the polders and resting after a delightful bicycle trip. There were quite a few of us in the party, and soon some of the group around me began to discuss a sermon we had heard the day before.

"I thought he made things much too simple," said one. "Becoming a child of God isn't that easy."

"But as many as received Him, to them gave He power to become the sons of God" (John 1:12).

"Yes, but before you receive Him, you must be elected."

"Certainly, but that is God's business. All you have to do is obey. If that were not possible it would not have been written 'work out your own salvation with fear and trembling' (Phil. 2:12). And though we do so at times with fear and trembling, the wonderful part of it is that ' it is God which worketh in you both to will and to do '. That means that we are on the victorious side because God is omnipotent.

" He Himself has given His only begotten Son to us that we might have eternal life ' who will have all men to be saved and to come unto the knowledge of the truth ' (I Tim. 2: 4).

" Jesus says, ' Come unto me, ALL ye that labour and are heavy laden, and I will give you rest ' (Matt. 11: 28).

" There are in the Bible two very important truths on this subject. One is that God rules over this universe and that He is omnipotent; that is God's sovereignty. The other is that we are held accountable; that is human responsibility. Logically, these two truths cannot be harmonized. They are like two ropes hanging from the ceiling not touching each other anywhere. Only if one should look above the ceiling would he see that they are connected and are actually the two ends of one rope.

" We must be careful not to do injustice to either of these truths of Scripture by the analysis of logic. St. Paul states it very clearly in I Corinthians 1 and 2. There are two planes or levels. One is that of the " wisdom of the wise ", the wisdom of this world. The other is that of the foolishness of God, which is wiser than the wisdom of the wise; this is the love of God that passes all understanding.

" We cannot and must not reduce the foolishness of God, which is the greatest wisdom, to the level of human wisdom. We may do the reverse. If, through the power of God's Spirit, we lift our logical thinking, which is the wisdom of the wise, to the plane of the foolishness of God, we see that His foolishness is not illogical but super-logical. We then enter the sphere of higher dimensions. God's thoughts are higher than our thoughts.

"We are able to comprehend these things only by faith, the substance of things hoped for, the evidence of things not seen. Faith is the radar which penetrates the clouds of our logical thinking and discerns the love of God which passes all understanding. Theology is the queen of sciences as long as it remains a tool in the hands of the Holy Spirit; but if it is used by man in order to raise barricades behind which he wishes to entrench himself, then it becomes theology in the hands of Satan.

"Now," I continued, "tell me honestly, when the minister spoke to you after the service and asked you, 'Won't you say "yes" to Jesus now, and surrender your life in obedience to Him', did you do it? No, you didn't, because that arrow glanced off your theological barrier. You knew very well that to lose your life for Christ's sake would mean to obey Him, and that would involve breaking with your sins, particularly with that one pet sin of yours. You didn't want to do that.

"And right at this point we come back to that glorious divine side of conversion. You realize eventually that you, yourself, cannot break with your sins; but if you turn over the reins of your life into the hands of Jesus Christ, you are at once on the victorious side. For

He ' was manifested that He might destroy the works of the devil ' (I John 3 : 8).

" Conversion is not, as some may think, a leap into the dark, but a leap into the light, straight into the arms of the Lord Jesus."

THE MANUFACTURER OF OUR FAITH

*It is not a great faith that we need, but faith in a
great God.*

I WAS back again in Germany. It was spring, and
people were building everywhere. Ruins were being cleared away. Property owners who did not
clear the rubble from their land would forfeit its owner-
ship. Everything was being done as cheaply as possible, no town planning with harmoniously constructed
neighbourhoods, no lovely homes with bay windows,
no beauty either within or without. The people just
built wherever they were, in the midst of the ruins,
and used old partially burnt or broken bricks. Here
and there the ruins themselves were merely patched
up, with no effort made to demolish and rebuild.
Rooms without exterior walls served as verandas or
even as storage space.

In the areas where rebuilding had not yet begun
there were shrubs growing in the midst of the ruins,
growing where once had been rooms, rooms where
people had lived.

Fresh young leaves were coming out on the branches,
and their colours were lovely in the spring sunlight.
The colours of ruins, too, can be lovely, but their forms
are horrible. That is why it was so terrifying to walk
in the streets at night.

I had just spoken to a group of young people on the

riches we have in Jesus Christ. Germans are very reserved; and when I invited them to remain for a period of discussion after the meeting, it took courage for the seven who accepted to overcome their instinctive reluctance to do so. Once so far, however, the ice was broken.

One of them said, " I am an atheist. You do it with Jesus; I do it without Him, and do at least as well as you." As he told me about his successes in his own strength, I said very little. Debating has never been one of my strong points. I prayed silently for him as I listened, and then said, " If the time should come in your life when you can no longer go on in your own strength, then remember and think about what you heard this evening."

Then another boy began to speak and said, "The Bible is for me an inventory record of all I possess in Him. I followed Hitler with all my heart and soul. But God intervened in my life and took everything away from me. I was a prisoner, and one of my comrades read the Bible with me every day we were in the prison camp. It was then that I came to know Jesus."

Tongues were loosened now, and others began to tell about their difficulties. One said, " I am so unfaithful; I want to believe, but my faith wavers. Now that you have told us all these things, I feel certain again; but what about tomorrow? I don't know whether it will be so then."

I told him that I was a watchmaker by trade, and that in our shop we received sometimes new watches that did not keep good time. These I did not repair myself, but sent back to the manufacturer. When he had repaired them, they ran accurately. And that is also what I do with my faith. Jesus is the "author and finisher of our faith". If there is something wrong with my faith I send it back to the heavenly manufacturer. When He has repaired it, it functions perfectly.

It is fortunate that Hebrews 12:2 does not read "Let us look unto our own faith."

If I should do that, I would perhaps say, "My faith is great." That would be pride, and the victory would be the devil's. Spiritual pride is very destructive.

Or if I should say, "Oh, my faith doesn't amount to anything; it doesn't do anything for me." That is defeatism; and it, too, is a victory of the devil.

Hudson Taylor once said, "We do not need a great faith, but faith in a great God."

Let us therefore look more and more to Jesus, and not upon our own faith. Let us look not upon the storms around us, but keep our eyes fixed upon Him. Then we shall be able to walk upon the waves of the turbulent sea of life. Faith is such a firm foundation that the safest place for a Christian to walk is the water that Peter trod as he went to meet Jesus.

Our conversation just naturally turned into prayer, and even the "atheist" folded his hands and closed his eyes.

INTERCESSORY PRAYER

Jesus Christ is able to untangle all the snarls in your soul, to banish all your complexes, and to transform even your fixed habit patterns, no matter how deeply they are etched in your subconscious.

MY technique of working has developed only gradually through experience. I prefer now to speak to the same people eight times, reserving forenoons for personal consultations, and having a period for discussion after every evening meeting.

In Germany it is not easy to get people to talk. They have had training in keeping silence. It was very dangerous for anyone to express an opinion during the Hitler regime. Now again there is fear, for to show one's colours these days may involve one in serious difficulties in the future.

So when I announced, " This meeting has now come to a close; but all those who would like to remain for a while to converse about these things are cordially invited to do so," it was merely the signal for emptying the church lecture-room within two minutes.

That was definitely not the right method, and I prayed for wisdom.

The next evening I clothed my invitation differently, saying, " The meeting has now come to an end, and we shall have a period of discussion. Will all of those who must or wish to leave, kindly do so at this time?"

Now it took courage for people to stand up and leave, and so they remained seated. When it had required courage to remain, they all left.

We had a very lively discussion. Questions came from all directions. And I prayed, "Lord, let me be only a channel for Thy Spirit; I am not equal to this."

Then I experienced a miracle. Even before a question had been completely stated, I already knew the answer.

I knew, of course, that such group discussions did not provide the real heart-to-heart contacts, so the morning hours for personal conferences were very important. It is when we are alone with people that we come close to them. And it was during these hours, more than anywhere else, that I could hear the cry of a wounded Germany.

This morning a woman came to my room. Her face was pale and embittered; about her head she had wrapped a black scarf. The Germans can sometimes display their misery in such a dramatic way.

It seemed to me that darkness entered the room with her, and I prayed, "Lord, cover me with Thy blood."

She began to speak in a complaining tone; and her sermon, like all good sermons, had three points. The subject of point one was how very bad people are in general, the Christians in particular, and the preachers worst of all! Point two was how very good she herself was: she talked about her virtues and the good deeds she had done. Then followed point three as conclusion. How is it possible that people dare to say that there is a God when such a good woman as herself should have so sad a life, such poor health, and so tiny a room in which to spend her days?

When she had finished she looked at me as if to say, " And now of course you will quote the Scriptures to me."

" I have a word for you," I said.

" Oh, have you?" I could see her thinking, " Here it comes "; but I said mischievously:

" Edel sei der Mensch, hilfreich und gut." (Let man be noble, helpful, and good.)   It was a quotation from Goethe, who is again greatly admired and faithfully read in a large part of Germany today.

The woman's reply was unexpected, " But I cannot fill my empty heart with that."

I looked at her in surprise.

But I had more to say to her, " Jesus has said, ' Come unto Me, all ye that labour and are heavy laden, and I will give you rest ' " (Matt. 11 : 28).   Then I gave her one rich promise after another from God's Word, and a miracle took place before my eyes.   The woman drank in every word thirstily, as though parched for the water of life.

Never before had I witnessed such a sudden change in attitude.   When she left the room, I knew she was a changed person, not yet a converted one, but a person who had opened her heart to the truth, and was eager to know more of it.

Immediately after she left, a gentleman entered the room and said, " I've already waited an hour to see you."

" I'm sorry; I didn't know you were here. But it would have been impossible to cut short our conversation."

" It is really quite all right," he replied, " I made good use of the time. I could hear snatches of your conversation from the next room and began to pray for you, for I realized you were having a hard time."

" When did you begin to pray?"

" Half an hour ago."

When the man began to pray, the miracle happened: the woman opened her heart to the Gospel.

How little we realize the great importance of intercessory prayer! If at this moment you pray for someone, even though he is on the other side of the globe, the Lord Jesus will touch him.

" I did not come to see you about myself," continued the man. " There is in this town a woman who is in great need, and I came to ask if you would perhaps try to contact her. She has refused to see any of us, though we have prayed much for her. You may succeed where we have failed."

" I would be very happy to try. What is her name and address?"

He mentioned her name. It was the name of the woman who had just left my room, and I exclaimed, " But that is the very woman who was here a few minutes ago! You will be able to reach her now, for she is longing to know more about the Gospel. You have prayed for her, and now you may thank God."

When we intercede for a person with God, we are participating in God's economy of salvation. This means nothing less than that we have opened our hearts to God's Spirit, who prays within us. Could that be the reason why it also operates within ourselves in such a saving, releasing way?

I once travelled by car through the mountains of California from Los Angeles to San Francisco. It is one of my weak points that I am afraid of driving through mountains with Americans. They usually drive at such great speed. Along one side of the road was a deep chasm, and, moreover, there were many dangerous curves. I knew from experience what to do when the demon of fear entered my heart. He had called on me many a time during my imprisonment in Germany, and I would then begin to sing. Singing always helps. Try it yourself some time; fear and anxiety will vanish when you sing.

So I sang one hymn after another, until my host, the driver, said teasingly, " Are you afraid?"

" Yes," I said, " that is why I am singing."

But this time it was all to no avail. Every time we approached a curve, I would think, " If another car is coming towards us from beyond that curve, we shall certainly crash into each other!" And, thoroughly frightened, I would stop singing.

No, singing did not help me now. Then I tried to dispel my fear by prayer, and I prayed. But my prayer became a refrain: " Lord, bring us safely to San Francisco. Do not let us crash down into this abyss. Please grant that there will be no car approaching us from around that curve ahead."

I kept on praying to dispel my fear, until suddenly, and I do not know how the idea came to me, I began to pray for others. I prayed for everyone who came into my thoughts, people with whom I had travelled, those who had been in prison with me, my school friends of years ago. I do not know how long I continued in prayer, but this I do know, my fear was gone. Interceding for others had released myself.

Some time ago in San Diego, I met a man who told a story of the power of intercessory prayer. He had been a heavy drinker, and was finally taken to a psychopathic hospital. Here he was placed in a room with three other patients, who did nothing but scream. When night came he was in despair. He prayed, but could not fall asleep while the screams continued. Then suddenly he began to pray for the three patients, and just as suddenly the screams ceased.

"Not only that," continued the man, "it seemed as if something broke in me. When I prayed for others, my own tension was released, and I was free. The next day I had to undergo a psychiatric examination. At its conclusion the doctor said, 'There is nothing wrong with you; you are normal.' I knew that night that I had become a free man."

Intercession often adds to its many other blessings the healing of one's own tension.

REFUGEES IN DISTRESS

O'er the ruin within, around us
Shines the star of Bethlehem.
In our sin and need it found us
And it led us to our King.
O'er the ruin within, around us
Heaven's light is shining still;
God in mercy has unbound us
From the night of Satan's will.

HUNDREDS of refugees were living in a big factory. The machinery had been taken away, but every corner of the building was in use, as living-quarters for the persecuted people who had found rest there.

Rest?

I was in a hall where about two hundred people were living together. It was like an enormous house without partitions. Around a table children were doing their school work. Behind them were beds, and behind the beds was still another " room ". Girls were getting ready to sleep. Farther on there lay men who had just returned from work. Dead tired, they had stretched out on the mattresses.

Most of the people had already lived there for three years. Though everyone was rather quiet at that moment, there was a murmur of many voices and the stir of a great number of people. There was no privacy, no room for anyone to call his own. It reminded me of a big waiting-room, but it was not that at all; people were not waiting here in order to leave; this was where they lived.

One could easily see the difference in degree of prosperity between the various family groups. Here in one place were beds with thick eiderdown quilts and elegant bedspreads, and a lamp with a lovely shade standing on a colourful Persian table cover. Right next to it there were a couple of mattresses on the floor with soiled blankets and without sheets. A woman was cutting black bread on a dirty wooden table.

The superintendent who showed me around the place said, " Now why don't you give these people a message? If I ask for silence all of them will be able to hear you."

But I shrank back, " Oh, no, please; not today," I begged. " I cannot speak here now. I would like to come back later on to live with them. Perhaps then I will dare approach them, but I can't just step in from the outside, to say a word, and then go back to my own peaceful guest-room."

After two months I returned. But I came at a bad time. There was a strong feeling of opposition toward all Christians. A minister had done a very stupid thing. He had visited the factory, and then written a newspaper article describing the situation there in very roseate terms. After reading his article one would almost be tempted to ask for permission to live in the factory, even though one had a small home of one's own. The occupants of the factory were justifiably indignant, not only with the minister in question, but with all Christians in general. As a result an evangelist who had worked there among the children had been refused admission. Moreover, a paper had been posted near the entrance stating that no one who called himself a Christian would be permitted to enter the place.

I did not allow myself to be intimidated by all this, but went to the police and inquired about the possibility of having myself registered as a refugee.

" But you are not a refugee," the police-officer said.

I explained the situation to him, and he was amused. I was registered, and shortly afterwards I walked into the factory right past the prohibitory paper.

The situation inside had improved. Ropes had been stretched from one wall to the other, and over the ropes were hung blankets or newspapers which had been sewn together and fastened to the lines by means of clothes-pins. In this way everyone now had at least something that resembled a room of his own. During the day I was to stay with a married couple; and sleeping arrangements were made on the other side of the " street ", where a bed had been placed for me in a little " room " occupied by two women. I was to do my own cooking, and had already bought some eggs and tomatoes. When I asked my hostess to lend me a pan, she called out, " Who will lend a frying-pan to the new-comer?"

A frying-pan appeared from under the blanket partition, and I went downstairs to the basement, which had been fitted up as a kitchen. The heat there was unbearable. Big stoves were going full blast, and around them women were doing their cooking, as many as forty of them around one stove.

It was interesting to see how the menus of the various nationalities differed from one another. The Germans as a rule cook starchy foods, many potatoes, sometimes with macaroni as substitute for vegetables, and followed by pancakes for dessert. There were women from Latvia, Poland, and Czechoslovakia, and all of them had different menus. My little meal of eggs and tomatoes, though rich in vitamins, was not regarded with appreciation, and certainly no one would have been willing to exchange food with me.

I left the over-heated kitchen as soon as possible and, in the company of my hostess, ate my first home-cooked dinner as a " refugee ". We sat on a little bench and ate from a box which served as a table. It cannot be denied that there was a certain atmosphere of snugness between the paper partitions, but the sounds and odours from all the other " apartments " penetrated unhindered into our " room ".

Then I started what was actually to be my work here. From one " room " to another I went " calling ". I talked little but listened much, and gazed into the depths of suffering and joyless existence. Most of the people were the discouraged ones, who no longer had enough energy to work themselves up from this level of existence. Dispirited and embittered at the same time, they told me about their flight from bombings, and their wanderings from one camp to another until they had here found their " home ".

Some of the people had adapted themselves amazingly well to their new surroundings. But such surroundings! Unemployed men and boys were playing cards in a bored sort of way. Women were trying to tidy up their " houses ". There was a nasty fishy smell in the building. Some women were doing their cooking, and odours of food mingled with those of cigarettes, cheap perfumes, jute, and other unpleasant scents. The sun burned down on the glazed roof. I lived on the attic floor, and its small windows were closed.

A little girl walked directly across our " room " toward her own " home ". She simply pushed the newspaper and blanket partitions aside.

Somewhere in the building a woman was screaming. She had come to get her daughter, who had been held here during the night. Whether it had been against her will or not, I was unable to find out. Things happened here just as they do in many quarters of the big cities where the poor, the unemployed, and the desperate live together. But the difference here was the sounds were unrestrained by partitions.

Everyone stopped talking and listened to hear the end of the row. After the woman had gone, life resumed its course and sounds: the whining of a mouthorgan, the complaining cry of a sick child, the snapping of an overstrung mother, the thumping of romping boys, and the uninterrupted buzzing of more than two hundred voices.

Was there any rest to be found in this place? I visited the people and tried to talk to them. I listened to their stories of misery and flight. " Would things ever become better in this world?" they asked me. I could speak only about the future of Jesus Christ, of His second coming and of the new earth wherein righteousness shall dwell. For this world I see so little hope left. There is only hope for this world in the light of I Peter 1:6, "Though now for a season, if need be, ye are in heaviness through manifold temptations." It is the light of Jesus Christ which continues to shine in the most profound darkness, the light which is victorious on behalf of those who know and love Him. To them, all things work together for good.

Was there still hope for this part of the world, where nine million refugees were crowded into the houses which still remained standing in this bombed-out land of ruins, for a country where the remaining factories were being blown up, where unemployment was increasing day by day, and where the means of subsistence had simply vanished?

I thanked God for my experiences in the concentration camp. Now I could tell these people about my experience of the reality of Jesus Christ in the hell of Ravensbruck. The fact that I also had suffered aroused their interest, and I was entitled to speak, because I could understand them.

In the evening my host came home. He borrowed a stool from the neighbours, and after supper two elderly men entered with their stools and, crowded together, they smoked their pipes in the little "newspaper room". I was tired to death when I lifted the "blanket door" of the neighbours, and entered their room to get ready to sleep. It was a good bed they had made up for me. As I stretched out on it, everything that I had experienced that day passed before my mind's eye like a film.

At Ravensbruck I had had good training in casting all my care and burden upon Him of whom it is said, "Cast all your care upon Him; for He careth for you" (I Peter 5:7). My suitcase of cares was full to the brim, and when I emptied it before the Lord I prayed, "Lord, here they are; help me now to leave them with Thee and continue my way unburdened."

There was noise all around me. What an unrest! Then suddenly out of the confusion of sounds around me a conversation struck my ear. On the other side of the paper partition two men were planning how they would deal with a Christian who might be bold enough to enter the building. I didn't hear the end of their discussion, because I was already asleep before they stopped talking. The last thought which came to mind before I fell asleep was "Underneath me are His eternal arms."

CHAIRS IN THE CAMP

" I will instruct thee and teach thee in the way which thou shalt go."—Psalm 32 : 8.

WHILE living in the factory I received an invitation from the Inter-varsity Christian Fellowship to work for ten months among its student groups in American colleges and universities.

Life in the factory had tired me out. It was the last one of the ten months that I intended to spend in Germany. The work there had been very gratifying, but at the same time very fatiguing. As I read the letter, a great longing arose in me to visit the United States. The Americans are less complex than the Germans. Of course, they have not come through such terrifying times.

I didn't know what to do. I wanted very much to go to the States, but I knew that if it was God's will for me to continue my work in Germany, He would also renew my strength. I only wanted to know where He was calling me.

So now I asked for a miracle, a sign. Was that permissible? Certainly: Gideon did.

" Lord, if it is Thy will that I should go to America, then grant me free passage. That will be sign to me. I know that Thou art willing to grant me money for the trip, but I cannot help thinking how many chairs I could buy for the camp at Darmstadt with that much money."

I knew now how uncomfortable it was to have no chairs. When my friends and I fitted out the camp at Darmstadt we did not have enough money to buy chairs. Beds, clothing, food, all of the barest necessities, we were able to procure, but we had no money for chairs.

When I talked these things over with my friends they said that it indicated that I should not go to America. Why not? God is a God of miracles. He would be able to grant me free passage.

I went to the office of a shipping company in Amsterdam. "I want to go to America," I said, "and would like to work for my passage as a stewardess." I could see some humour in the situation, for, after all, I was no longer very young, and it was questionable whether I would be able to do such work.

"Do you know that stewardesses are allowed to spend only one week in America? They have to return on the same boat."

"Oh, no. I intend to stay in the United States for ten or eleven months. But will you allow me to tell you something about my life story?" I asked. "During the war——"

"Wait, you don't have to say another word. I know all about it. Here is your book, 'A Prisoner and Yet . . .'; I know your entire story. Isn't it wonderful that God actually called you to work in Germany?"

"Yes, it certainly is, but how do you know about that?"

"I have always been interested in your activities, and it will not be my fault if you don't succeed in obtaining free passage."

He arranged everything for me. I was to travel on a freighter, presumably as a stewardess.

The occupants of my camp at Darmstadt got their chairs, and the most wonderful thing about it as far as I was concerned was the assurance that it was God's will and His guidance that I should go to America.

HOLLYWOOD

" But as many as received Him, to them gave He power to become the sons of God, even to them that believe on His name."—John 1 : 12.

I HAD been invited to attend the meeting of a prayer group of film stars in Hollywood; and I was excited, waiting to see what would happen.

It was indeed a group of fine-looking people. They received me cordially but very informally, and at first I felt a bit out of my element.

After one of them had read the scriptures to us, they all knelt down, and I was moved as I observed a gladness and thankfulness in their prayers such as I had seldom witnessed before. When I spoke to them I found them open-minded, and afterwards some of them told of their experiences. " I was so happy when I got to know the Lord Jesus," one of them said. "That week I had to play a dramatic part in which I was supposed to cry. I simply could not cry. I was too happy."

Some of the stars told of their " suffering shame for His sake ". Like many other Christians in the United States, they abstain from drinking and smoking. Therefore it soon became known that they were Christians, and people asked them: " Don't you smoke? Are you a member of a Sunday school?"

Then when they professed their faith courageously, they sometimes had to face derision and contempt from their colleagues.

A young and pretty girl named Colleen Townsend said to me: " I'll remain in the film-world until God makes it clear to me that I must leave it. We are the only people who can approach our colleagues, and we want to make use of our opportunities as long as possible."

Three weeks later I read in the paper that she had resigned from her very lucrative job and had become a Bible-school student.

The second time I came into contact with this group was at their Gospel meeting which was held every two weeks for their non-Christian colleagues. The meeting was held in the home of Jane Russell.

Her house is really extraordinary. It is situated on top of a mountain, and the last part of the road to it is so steep that it is accessible only by car. One wall of the living-room is made entirely of glass, and from this vantage point there is a magnificent view of Hollywood. The structure of the room and the furniture are most unusual, and have a decided charm.

A young minister spoke that evening, and brought his message of sin and salvation with great earnestness but interspersed with real humour. He showed that the greatest of all sins is unbelief and the will to resist Jesus Christ. Not only the demand of conversion, but also the great joy of being a child of God, he proclaimed in such a way that it really inspired his entire audience. With no hesitation whatever he described the future of those who are lost, an eternity without Jesus Christ.

Sing-Sing and Hollywood. The extreme east and the extreme west of the United States. Nowhere else have I witnessed such an interest in and open-mindedness for the Glad Tidings.

Later in Holland, when delivering a lecture on America, I told my audience about this experience in Hollywood. During the discussion someone asked me: "How is it possible to be a film star and a Christian at the same time?"

I prayed for wisdom to answer that question, and then said, "To combine the frivolous life of a film star with Christianity is practically impossible. But equally impossible are the combinations of pride and Christianity, self-sufficiency and Christianity, irreconcilability and Christianity, back-biting and Christianity."

It reminds me of the story of Jesus and the adulterous woman. "He that is without sin among you, let him first cast a stone at her" (John 8 : 7). And Jesus Christ is very serious in His command to the film stars and to all decent and indecent sinners: "Go, and sin no more" (John 8 : 11).

How wonderful it is that He came into this world to save sinners! On Calvary we see the awful sinfulness of sin, but we also behold Him, "The Son of God who was manifested that He might destroy the works of the devil" (I John 3 : 8).

"For we are His workmanship, created in Christ

Jesus unto good works, which God hath before ordained that we should walk in them " (Eph. 2 : 10).

When we are hidden with Christ in God, then we are on the victorious side.

IN LONDON

" God is willing to enter into the heart, as light is willing to flood a room that is opened to its brightness."—Amy Carmichael.

IN London I was asked to call on a woman in a mental institution. The one who had fallen a victim to hatred. She had always lived in Palestine. Her husband had been kind to the Jews, and then it was the Jews who had dropped a bomb on their home. When she regained consciousness and saw that her husband was dead, she opened her heart to hatred. Now she was a complete wreck. She spent the whole day reading the newspapers in order to find news about the Jews. If something terrible happened to them she was happy.

Poor woman!

As she entered the room she looked suspiciously at me. I prayed for wisdom and love.

" I know exactly what you're going to tell me. I must pray," she began the conversation in a defiant manner. " But I cannot pray."

I made no reply, and she continued, " I know exactly what you are going to say next; I must banish the hatred from my heart, because only then can I pray again."

" Who has told you that?"

" The chaplain."

" No doubt the chaplain is still a very young man, and he does not yet know how powerful the devil of hatred is. You and I know. Once I was with my sister in a concentration camp. When they treated me cruelly I could stand it, but when I saw that they intended to beat my sister, because she was too weak to shovel sand, then hatred tried to enter my heart. And then I experienced a miracle. Jesus had planted His love in my heart, and there was no room left for hatred. The only thing you can do is to open your heart to that love. That love is a reality. If it is dark in a room, while the sun is shining outside, do I have to sweep the darkness out? Of course not. I merely have to draw the curtains aside, and as soon as the sunlight floods the room the darkness vanishes."

We both knelt down, and I prayed, " Lord, here we are, weak, much weaker than the devil of hatred. But Thou art stronger than the devil of hatred, and now we open our hearts to Thee, and we give thanks to Thee that Thou art willing to enter into our hearts, as the sun is willing to flood a room that is opened to its brightness."

A week later the woman was discharged from the mental institution. Her heart was full of the love of God.

MAY

" For this purpose the Son of God was manifested, that He might destroy the works of the devil."—I John 3:8.

IN the middle of the woods was a little summer house. May and I were taking a walk along the cliffs near Lynton on the west coast of England. We had heard the day before an impressive lecture on the demand of unconditional surrender to God.

We rested in the summer house for a little, and May used the time to scoff at the lecture. Not only the content but the structure too was given a thorough going over. May just tore the lecture to shreds. I looked at her, and couldn't help smiling.

" What is the reason for all these objections? Is it perhaps because you do not want to do what is demanded of you? Have you ever surrendered completely? In John 3 we read the story of a man who came to Jesus. He was told that ' except a man be born again, he cannot see the kingdom of God, neither can he enter into it '. Has that ' being born of God's Spirit ' already taken place in your life?

" God's Spirit is here, He wants to dwell in you, but you have to make the choice. Does that seem so difficult? Not so long ago it was a choice between Jesus and a world of progressive and expanding civilization. Now it is a choice between Jesus and a world of rapid decline.

"You can make it seem very complicated, but isn't it much like a proposal of marriage? What kind of answer does a young man expect when he asks a girl to marry him? Certainly either yes or no; there is no other possibility. So it is when we choose between Jesus and the world. Jesus says, 'Come unto me', but your answer is 'No', because there is something behind your criticism, isn't there?"

"Just the same, I would like to surrender to Jesus," she said. "My whole heart is longing for peace with God. Actually I know the way, but when I am on the point of saying 'yes' a barrier seems to arise and keep me from surrendering."

"Listen, May. Think back over the events of your life and tell me if you have ever been in touch with spiritism. Have you ever been to a fortune-teller? Do you know that when you do such a thing you fall under the spell of it, through which the way to God becomes barred for you? Yes, even the way to conversion. Such a spell may ensnare you even if you have just allowed yourself to be treated by a mesmerist. Very often such people are also on the wrong side, and that may be a great danger."

May laughed in a mocking way. "As a matter of fact, I did allow myself to be persuaded to go to a fortune-teller years ago," she said, "but I did not believe in it, I did it only for fun. Afterwards we had a good laugh about it. I had completely forgotten about it, but now that you ask me, I remember it very well. But surely, there's no harm done, I did not believe a bit of it."

" May, suppose you were a soldier during a war and you had to reconnoitre a certain terrain. By mistake you fell into the enemy's hands by entering his territory. Do you think that it would help if you then said, ' Oh, excuse me, please, it was not my intention to come here; I just came here by mistake?' Once you are on their terrain, you are at their mercy. Though you did not know it, a demon has taken possession of your heart, and your life has fallen under his spell. When you want to be converted he comes in between. You don't understand the significance of it, and that's why it is so dangerous. St. Paul says in Ephesians 6: 12, ' For we wrestle not against flesh and blood, but against principalities, against powers.' "

The look of amusement had left May's face, and fear was there instead.

" I'm not telling you these things to make you afraid, May. If I had no more to say than this it would have been better to keep silent, but the first step toward victory is to know the enemy's position. And the wonderful thing about it is that Jesus is the victor. He is far stronger than all the powers of hell. What you have to do is to close the door exactly there where you opened it. I mean this; think of one of the scripture passages which speaks of forgiveness."

May thought for a moment, and then said, " Col. 1: 14, ' In His dear Son we have redemption through His blood, even the forgiveness of sins.' "

" That is right. Now ask the Lord Jesus to go back with you to that very moment when you committed that sin. Confess your sin, ask forgiveness, and give thanks for it, because the text, which you quoted, is true. Then the door is closed and you are free. Then you are no longer at the demon's mercy.

" I myself once had the opportunity of showing the way of salvation to a fortune-teller. It was in Germany. The whole day long she was busy ' closing doors '. Then she came back to me and said, ' I feel happier, but I know that there are sins which I have forgotten. I am not completely free yet.' "

" ' Just tell the Lord Jesus about it as you did to me and give thanks for forgiveness, ' " I replied.

" Two days later she returned and said, ' This morning I awoke singing: I am completely free.' She was full of praise and thanksgiving to the Lord.

" Will you do it too, May? I know for a certainty that you'll be victorious. I'll leave you to yourself now. Fight it out the rest of the way without me."

I left her alone and walked back to the conference grounds. The surf was pounding against the cliffs. A storm was coming up, and it was a tremendous sight. Near the shore a steep rock rose abruptly out of the sea. It was as if two powers fought against each other, but the rock stood unmoved amidst the waves.

On the last night of the conference the leader asked if any would tell what they had learned and experienced these weeks. May stood up and said, " I have learned and experienced here that Jesus is victor."

SWITZERLAND

It is foolish to underestimate the power of Satan, but it is fatal to overestimate it.

I HAD the privilege of speaking for three successive evenings in a little church built against the slope of a mountain in Switzerland. I was a guest in the beautiful manse, and enjoyed the conversation with the minister, the splendid view from my bedroom window, and the pure mountain air.

On the last evening I spoke on the reality of the promises of God. Often we do not understand these promises. They seem too lofty and beyond our comprehension, and so we lay them aside without really giving them serious thought. But that is not God's intention. He is back of every promise with His love and His omnipotence, and He was in great earnest when He made them. Therefore I believe that we are sinning when we ignore them or perhaps evade them by theologizing them away.

My train was not leaving until the following evening, and so the next afternoon found me standing outside the manse gazing at the beautiful panorama spread out before me. Far in the distance were snow-clad mountain-tops, and in front of them rose the green slopes of the foothills. The sky was bright blue, birds were singing exuberantly; and I myself was humming a hymn of praise to my Creator: " Never can faith expect too much."

Callers arrived to see me; a mother and her fifteen-year-old daughter. The child was a pitiful sight, for she cringed in fear at the slightest sound and buried her face in her mother's arm. The mother's face was full of sorrow as she looked at me pleadingly.

" You spoke last night on the reality of the promises of God," she said. " Do you believe that yourself?"

" Yes I do," I answered instantly. " God's promises are a greater reality than our problems."

" Then for Christ's sake cast out this demon," she said vehemently.

I shrank back as though she had struck me. Anything, but not that! That was a terrain on which I did not want to venture. Other people might be able to do so, but not I.

I prayed silently and asked, " Lord, you know that I cannot and will not do this."

The Lord answered me clearly and unmistakably. " But you must do it, because there is even more truth in what you just said to the woman than you yourself realize. My promises are true."

The mother and I read Mark 16, and then we prayed together and asked Jesus Christ to cover us with His blood, and give safe protection in every struggle against, or attack of, the devil.

I asked the child, " Do you know the Lord Jesus?"

" Yes," she said, " but I wish He would make me happy. I want to be happy."

Then I spoke to the demon, in the name of the Lord

Jesus, who has gained the victory on the Cross and who has cleansed us with His blood. In his Name I commanded the demon to come out of the girl and to go back to hell, where he belonged. I forbade him to enter anyone else or to possess the child again.

The poor girl left the manse as much possessed as when she came, and I was profoundly unhappy. How weak I was in faith, and how lacking in power! Was it only theory that I had been preaching, theory that failed when I tried to put it into practice?

I knocked on the door of the minister's study. He received me kindly. " I need your help," I said. " My faith was too small, and now you will have to do it," and I told him about my experience.

He looked up at me, startled, and said, " Oh, that is a sphere I refuse to enter."

" But who must do it then? You are the shepherd of this flock, and you have God's promises. Please, read St. Mark 16: 17."

He took his Bible and read, " And these signs shall follow them that believe; in My name shall they cast out devils." And verse 20: " And they went forth, and preached everywhere, the Lord working with them, and confirming the word with signs following."

The minister buried his face in his hands. His reading changed to prayer, and I heard him whisper, " Forgive me, Lord, that I have neglected my duty."

Great joy entered my heart. This was the reason I had to experience the failure of my own attempt. This shepherd had to learn something, and God used me as His instrument.

When I left in the evening there was no darkness, but only gratitude in my heart. There was still much that I didn't understand, but everything was all right.

Jesus is Victor.

Two days later I received a letter from the manse, " Corrie, something wonderful has happened. When the mother and her daughter crossed the threshold of their home the demon went out of the child. This morning both of them came to me full of praise and thanksgiving to Him who was really serious about the promises He made to us in the Scripture. My husband wants to know if you will come again, and this time stay longer than three days."

But I knew that this would not be necessary. JESUS is Victor, and He uses everyone who is willing to obey Him.

> Whate'er the love of God would do
> Is never by His power denied.

UNPAID DEBTS

We rob the work of Jesus Christ of its efficacy, and we stand powerless before the adversary, because we doubt the integrity of the Word of God.

A YOUNG minister was taking me to the station. I learn so much in conversation with people. I wish that everyone who works at spreading the Gospel could travel as I do, for it is a daily source of knowledge to meet so many people. One does not accept everything he hears, of course, any more than he accepts all that he reads in books. But as in eating fish one picks out the meat and lays aside the bones, so also in conversation; and one learns much in the process.

We had had a blessed meeting. God's Spirit had been at work, and now I asked the minister whether he had any scruples about the message. There are not many people who are willing to be frank enough to criticize the message of another, but it is just through such honest criticism that one learns most.

" Now that you ask me," he replied, " I will tell you. I thought your message was good, but I didn't like your terminology. You spoke on the Blood of Jesus. That is a term I should prefer to leave to the sects."

Though we had met only recently, I still felt sufficiently free to correct this young man and said, " You are in worse company than I am. The devil has a great aversion for that very term; in fact, he hates it

even more than you do. I am in better company, that
of the apostles Paul, John, and Peter. And, do you
know, as I looked around in your church I saw many
who were under the curse of evil powers?"

" Not merely under a curse!" he exclaimed, " Many
in my congregation are possessed by demons. It is
terrible, and I am powerless against it."

" Isn't it possible that your lack of power is a direct
result of your suppressing this important doctrine of the
Bible's message? We read in Revelation 12:11, ' And
they overcame him (the devil) by the Blood of the
Lamb.' Let us take joyously the sword of the Spirit,
which is the Word of God: and let us not weaken our
position by using only that which is beautiful and
attractive to us in the Bible or what we can accept on
the basis of reason."

We continued our talk for a long time; and when the
train was on the point of leaving he said laughingly,
" Perhaps there is some truth in the statement that the
sects are often the unpaid debts of the church."

BERMUDA

" He that abideth in Me, and I in him, the same bringeth forth much fruit; for without Me ye can do nothing."—John 15:5.

THERE was a woman tourist in Bermuda who used her vacation time not only for rest and recreation but also for spreading the Gospel. It was a time of great blessing for her, and after returning to her home in Jenkintown, she was faithful in intercession for the people living in that beautiful island. Together with her prayer group, she prayed that many of them would accept the Gospel.

Is there any better preparation for revival than that of a group of people praying with one accord? Can there be work more important than intercessory prayer?

It was during a visit to this friend that she asked me if I could arrange to go to Bermuda for a week. As far as time was concerned, it was possible to add it to my schedule. But I did not have money for the plane trip. So I asked the Lord for guidance. When it became clear that He wanted me to go, I wrote immediately to Bermuda saying that I would come; the matter of money I entrusted to the Lord. Within two or three days, cheques arrived from different people, people who knew nothing of the proposed trip. And there was just enough money for a return ticket.

The plane was approaching land.

The grey water beneath us turned to blue, as if a huge ink-well had been emptied into the sea. I saw white houses and a lot of green, and as we came down, gorgeously coloured flowers everywhere.

What a beautiful bit of land! The setting sun added brilliance to the many colours.

Customs officers, clad in white uniforms, searched our luggage. One of them looked at my papers and said, " Miss ten Boom, I'll take care of you as quickly as possible, because our prayer group is waiting for you. Then we'll go right over." This was a promising welcome: from the airport directly to a prayer meeting! It looked as though this would be a week full of action.

And it was! At the prayer group that evening there was evidence of great interest, a genuine thankfulness for the message, and a desire to know more about the Gospel. It was the beginning of a week of blessing such as I had never experienced before.

My schedule was more than filled. There were at least twenty speaking engagements, and there was scarcely any time for preparation between the successive addresses. I could not, nor would I, object, for I had asked them to give me as many opportunities as possible in order to make the most of my visit. I ran short of sleep because the post-meeting discussions often lasted far into the evening. Sometimes, however, I could sleep a few minutes between gatherings.

Whenever I spoke, I would ask all who were willing and able to pray during the meeting that God would make me an open channel for His Word, and that His

Spirit would work in the hearts of the people.   I felt myself upheld also by the prayers of my friends in the United States, who were in sympathy with me and who expected much of this work.

The very first morning a young man came to interview me for the Press. We found it possible to pray together, and he became an important and loyal helper in the work.   He was present at all twenty meetings, and each day there was an excellent and accurate report of my messages.   The result was that my talks became known to many who had not been to any of the meetings, and that in turn created possibilities for other less-formal contacts.

The work was quite varied, and took me from a nursery school class of the cutest coloured children to a dignified Rotary Club meeting, from the island prisons to its churches.   And in between were many conversations, sometimes on the street, or in stores or offices.

On the narrow winding roads my " manager " drove me from one place to another.   Traffic keeps to the left, of course, since Bermuda is English territory; and cars are not allowed to travel faster than twenty miles an hour.   But on this island there is time enough for everything.

As the car pulled up at our destination, a coloured man walked over and said, " I never knew that there were real children of God among the white people, but since our prayer meeting I know better."   And then he added, " God gave you a good training in your work among the feeble-minded in Holland.   Now you speak so simply that all of us can understand you."   I myself had often thanked God for that part of my experience, but it surprised me that this man had observed the importance of it so quickly.

My talk to the Rotary Club was broadcast over the radio, and in it I paid the Press a compliment, saying, " I have often read the greatest nonsense about myself in the newspapers. One time, for example, I read that I had released thirty-five thousand prisoners in Germany. Here in Bermuda, however, the Press is excellent. The main points of my talks are very correctly reported. I have been in many places, but nowhere else have the news reports been so good as here."

Next day a headline on the front page of the daily paper announced in big letters: " Corrie ten Boom says Bermuda has the best reporters in the world." But the nice part of it was that they now put forth even more effort than before to give me good publicity.

So everything worked together for good. God's Spirit was busy in the hearts of people. The messages that made the greatest impression were these: that the problem of sin has been solved on the Cross; that the devils and demons are conquered spirits; and that our struggle is a struggle of faith, through which we come to see the victory of Christ.

It was a great privilege to preach these Glad Tidings also in the prisons. Something happened there among the prisoners. The first time I spoke, one man stood up and said, " Come back again. We understand you and love to hear the things you tell. Please come again. We are not as bad as some people think." I was permitted to speak several times, and the prisoners were also allowed to hear my four radio addresses. So we learned to know one another quickly. The last time I visited them one prisoner arose and asked, " May we sing, ' Just as I am, O Lamb of God, I come '?" " Yes," I replied, " but only those who will truly come to the Saviour either for the first time or for recommitment." As long as I live I shall not forget the faces of those men as they sang, deeply moved, earnestly, yet joyously, " O Lamb of God, I come ". Before the second stanza, I said, " Now only those who wish to possess the fullness of God's Spirit." And then again, " Now sing it as a testimony to your neighbour."

Afterwards, a rough-looking man with unshaven face came up and presented me with a small cedar box. He had worked on it for months. Another prisoner pressed my hand and said, " I am a child of God."

The warden told me that the prisoners talked all day about what they had heard.

After this visit there was a final meeting in the church. My first talk had been the Sunday before to a handful of people in a basement room. Now the church was filled with both white and coloured people, something that is said to be unusual in Bermuda. The coloured sisters and brothers could not restrain their joy. Their " Hallelujah's " and " Praise the Lord's " resounded through the church. In conclusion, I announced the same hymn the prisoners had sung, " Just as I am, O Lamb of God, I come ". I told the audience what had happened in the prison, and added, " They who do not sing this straight from their hearts will be preceded by the prisoners in the kingdom of God." I knew that the prisoners were listening, because this final meeting was also being broadcast. And what a meeting it was!

Afterwards a white woman came up to me and said, "Do you suppose this is the beginning of the revival for which we have been praying so long?"

Bermuda, an island of great natural beauty, with colours everywhere! Deep-blue water, trees with brilliantly coloured blossoms, fields full of lilies, white houses. Bermuda, an island of friendly people. Some of them had taken me to a store and said, "Now you must buy something for yourself. No, this money must be spent on something for you. We won't allow you to use it for the work in Europe." Then they debated what would be beautiful enough for me.

Suddenly there flashed into my mind a picture from the past. As a despised prisoner in Scheveningen I had not been permitted the luxury of walking on the corridor runner. It was too good for me, though it was nothing but a coarse coco-mat; I had to walk alongside of it. Grey, colourless prison! Was God favouring me especially now in giving me the enjoyment of the gay and brilliant colours of this paradise and majestic island far out in mid-ocean, and the love of these warm-hearted islanders?

What has been the happiest experience of this blessed week? Just this: the privilege of dispensing the great riches of God's Word to people who do not tire of listening to it, to people who are hungering for the Gospel and never become satiated with it; to be allowed to speak from early morning until late in the evening about the promises of God, which are greater and have greater reality than our problems; to speak of the love that He requires of us but which He Himself supplies to us. And I prayed, "O Lord, do let me have more such experiences as this one. I want to work obediently only where you call me; but do call me to places where people are as hungry for the Gospel as in Bermuda, and where I may dispense as lavishly of Thy great riches. It is so wonderful to be able to share abundantly with others. O Lord, who am I, to have been so privileged? Thank you, Father, for these eight days, the most wonderful days of all my four years of travelling."

Then came Cleveland. I was staying with dear friends of mine, but there was not much opportunity for me to speak in their church: one evening meeting, poorly attended; and then I was allowed to speak for fifteen minutes to the children in the Sunday school. And I was discontented. Only a Sunday school! No, compared with this, Bermuda knew how to appreciate Corrie ten Boom.

What a success for the devil! Just imagine! The Lord Jesus stayed up half the night for one man, Nicodemus, and He considered it important enough to explain the most beautiful part of the Gospel to this one man. See John 3! But I didn't think it worthwhile to preach the Word to a group of children, children, with their whole lives still before them, children whose roots are not yet so deeply planted in the earth as those of adults. Young saplings are so much easier to bend than old tree-trunks. But pride had found its way into my heart. And right there things began to go awry—and though the beginning of a path be ever so slightly awry, its end will be far afield.

Chicago was next on my schedule, but no word had come to confirm my appointments there. I therefore decided, without waiting for guidance, that it was just as well to go a day later. Moreover, there were some unexpected opportunities to speak in Cleveland, so I sent a telegram to Chicago to inform them that I would arrive two days later.

A friend was waiting at the station in Chicago when I arrived.

" Why didn't you come at the appointed time?" was his first question. " You have missed two important engagements."

Startled, and also a bit chagrined, I answered, " Why didn't you write and confirm our arrangements?"

" We couldn't; you failed to send us your Cleveland address."

How ashamed I was!

Everything in Chicago went farther and farther awry. I missed connections and seemed to do the wrong thing at every turn. I was glad when the time came for me to leave for Holland, Michigan.

The first evening with my friends there we talked and talked.

" How was Bermuda?"

" Oh, wonderful! What a place! Such lovely people! And how hungry they are for the Word of God! It is so beautiful there, whole fields of lilies, flowering trees, deep-blue sea——!"

" And how was Cleveland?"

" Oh, nothing out of the ordinary."   And I began quickly to speak again about Bermuda.

" And Chicago?"

" An awful place to be in summer.   Stiflingly hot, both night and day.   No, give me Bermuda."

That evening I had a long talk with the Lord.   I had often said to people, " If there is a shadow somewhere in your past of which you do not like to be reminded, stop where you are and take it to God in prayer.   Ask Him to retrace your steps with you to that dark spot, ' For the blood of Jesus Christ cleanseth from all sin ', and His presence changes the darkness into light." Now it was my turn to put the precept into practice, and I prayed, " Lord, go back with me to Chicago and Cleveland.   What was wrong there?"

The answer was very clear: " Cleveland and Chicago, that was Corrie ten Boom without Me.   Bermuda, that was Corrie with Me."

Now I could see it.   What a privilege it is to see the reality of things!   Yes, the reality of our own sins, and unworthiness, and inadequacy—but in the light of the victory of Christ.

" Without Me ye can do nothing," said the Lord. " I can do all things through Christ who strengthens me," said Paul (Phil. 4 : 13).

The branch of the vine, without Him, bears no fruit at all, but with Him, much fruit, even an hundredfold.

FINANCES

His is the gold and silver of the whole earth, the cattle on a thousand hills.

ON my early trips to the United States I used to speak at times on the need in the Netherlands and Germany, and on the work which we do there, and then ask that people support our work financially.

In general, Americans are very liberal. The many parcels they have sent to the poverty-stricken countries of Europe during the post-war years bear witness to their liberality; and those parcels, in the great majority of cases, did not come from the wealthy. I have often been present when American housewives were preparing such parcels. Every time they went shopping they bought something for Europe, and these purchases were set aside in a specially reserved place. I wonder if they used their "tithe" for this? Many Christians place a tenth of their income aside for the work of God, and they remain faithful in this even in times of scarcity.

Preparing these parcels is not an easy job! There are many forms to fill out; and the weights and measures of the parcels have to meet certain requirements. Only then is the parcel taken to the post office.

"Thank goodness, that package is off! And fortunately it was not too heavy!" the tired housewife exclaims. Then they continue—how often I've heard them: " But I'm so glad to be able to do something for the people of Europe who are living under such trying conditions."

It has really been quite a job. As a rule American housewives have no easy life. They are often employed outside the home also in order to earn extra money, and their evenings are frequently taken up with endless church and social gatherings. Many people in Europe think that all Americans are wealthy, but that is not true. Generally they have to work as hard as anywhere else in the world to keep their heads above water.

People in America do not seem to think it strange when a speaker from Europe asks for a collection to be taken for the work there, but I myself sometimes felt that there was something wrong about it.

I had been speaking on the need in the Netherlands and in Germany, and after the meeting a dignified and well-dressed woman came up to give me a sum of money for the work in these countries.

" It was so very interesting to hear about your work," she said.

" What did you think about the other things of which I spoke? Did you find them important also?" I asked. " Of course it is a very good thing to give money for evangelistic work, but today I spoke also on conversion. God does not want only a little of our money, He wants our hearts. Because of His great love He wants to possess you completely. The Lord Jesus wants you to come to Him with all your cares, with all your sins, with all your unrest concerning the past, with all your fears about the future. He says: 'I will give you rest'. Let Him hold the reins of your life. Then you will understand that His yoke is easy and His burden light, and then His joy will fill your heart; for it is His intention 'that His joy might remain in you, and that your joy might be full ' " (John 15 : 11).

While I was speaking there came a haughty look into her eyes. Very coolly, she took her leave with no response whatsoever to my comments.

When I got back to my room I looked sadly at the money she had given me. Was there perhaps something wrong in speaking of one's own work and at the same time on the need of conversion? When I prayed about it the answer was very clear: " From now on you must never again ask for money."

Great joy entered my heart, and I prayed: " Heavenly Father, Thou knowest that I need more money than ever before, not only for travelling expenses and for the house in Holland, but also for the camp in Germany. But from now on the little evangelization work of the ' ten Boom Foundation ' will be carried out on the same basis as the great mission work of Hudson Taylor. I know that Thou wilt never forsake us."

That day I received two letters. One was from a woman in Switzerland. " Corrie, God told me that from now on you must never ask for money again," she wrote. The other letter was from my sister in Holland. She wrote: " When I prayed for your work this morning God made it very clear to me that you should not ask anybody for financial support. He will provide everything."

I thought of the night in the concentration camp when my sister Bep and I had talked about our plans. " Corrie, we should never waste our energy in collecting money. God is willing to supply our every need."

And now this repeated charge, in Switzerland to my friend, in Holland to my sister, and here in the United States to me. God takes his prohibition of asking for money seriously, just as He means it seriously that He will care for and protect us. He is willing and able to supply our every need according to His own riches; we may trust in that promise one hundred per cent.

THE SECOND COMING

" Then we which are alive and remain shall be caught up together with them in the clouds, to meet the Lord in the air, and so shall we ever be with the Lord."—I Thess. 4:17.

WE were sitting in a park under the shadow of a large tree. A conference was being held in the stately house behind us, but today the weather was so beautiful that we could have our meeting out in the park. The view of the lake, with a dense forest in the distance, was lovely.

Our gathering at this time was not an official one.

I had mentioned a couple of times in my lectures the second coming of the Lord Jesus, and several people had expressed a desire to know more about this subject. So I offered to tell them what I knew about the subject some time between our scheduled sessions.

I began by giving them an illustration: " A telephone operator was called each day by the same person and asked for the time. After some months of this she asked the inquirer for the reason of his daily call. ' At twelve sharp I have to give a whistle signal,' the man said. Startled, the girl answered, ' And I always set my watch by that very whistle signal.' "

That is the world today. There is no foundation, no certainty, no safe objective standard.

The Bible, however, is our Standard time.

" Give me a place outside the earth on which to rest my lever and I will move the world," Archimedes said.

We possess this " Archimedes' fulcrum " in the Word of God.

The great blessing of our time is that the world is aware of the fact that it is bankrupt. The widespread middle-class contentment, which gave the world its false sense of security up to forty years ago, has vanished. The whistle signal has deviated too much from true time, and as a result people have lost confidence in it. These are the days in which the trumpet of every Christian must sound no uncertain note.

The world complains that there is no longer a future. But we find in the Bible that one out of every twenty-five texts speaks of the assured future of the kingdom of God at the coming of His Son. There is no one who fears His coming so much as the devil; and it has been a victory of the devil that the greatest consolation which the Bible grants us has been changed into a subject of theological controversy.

Jesus Himself, Paul, Peter, and John, all state in unmistakable language that there will be a point in time at which Jesus will return. This momentous event will be so glorious to them who belong to Him that it is written, " Wherefore comfort one another with these words." Then they will be with the Lord forever. To those who do not love Him there will be judgment and tribulation. It is very clearly written, " But exhort one another daily."

There will be signs of the times, of which we must be observant. To those who do not belong to Him Jesus will come " as a thief in the night ", but the children of God " are not in darkness, that that day should overtake them as a thief " (I Thess. 5 : 2, 4).

One of the most outstanding signs of the times is the return of the Jews to the land of Israel. Frederick the Great of Prussia once said, " If one wants to know the time on the clock of world history, let him observe the Jews."

Our confession of faith speaks of the second coming of Christ only as the judgment of the living and the dead. To those who are in Christ this judgment will be the glorious moment in which they will be manifested as the redeemed.

To the world the second coming of Christ will mean the end of Satan's dominion over the world, the end of the rule of the prince of this world. For Jesus is coming to take possession of His own inheritance. It will be an invasion by the Owner Himself who has promised: " Behold, I make all things new " (Rev. 21:5). Then " the earth shall be filled with the knowledge of the glory of the Lord, as the waters cover the sea " (Hab. 2 : 14). Therefore, those who love His appearing, pray with St. John, " Even so, come, Lord Jesus " (Rev. 22 : 20).

" But I don't understand anything of all that I am hearing," said a young woman. The other listeners, too, admitted that this was unfamiliar territory to them. Yet this conference was not being held for unchurched laymen. All of these people were attending the conference because they desired, more or less, to discuss and to be trained in the methods of proclaiming the

Gospel in their own surroundings. To these convinced Christians, the second coming of Christ was totally unfamiliar ground.

" When the Son of man cometh, shall He find faith on the earth?" (Luke 18 : 8).

TWO LITTLE GIRLS

The Bible is not a frozen bank account.

A MOTHER whom I was visiting brought two little girls about ten years of age to me. One of the girls was her own daughter, the other her foster child.

"Will you tell them how to become children of God?" she asked. "Both of them attend Sunday school; they know something of the Bible, but over and over again they ask me, 'How can I become a child of God?' I don't know how to explain that to them."

We were in a village high in the mountains of Switzerland. The small house was on the edge of the village, and there was a beautiful view of the Alps.

I prayed to the Lord for wisdom. We have the promise in James 1:5, "If any of you lack wisdom, let him ask of God, that giveth to all men liberally." God's promises are true. I have an idea that God is pleased when we confront Him with His promises; He then knows that we have faith.

I sat down with the two girls on a bench in front of the house. "Now look," I said. "Just suppose that I wanted to adopt one of you as my child. That wouldn't be easy. First of all I'd have to fill out many papers. It would take a long time before everything was in order. But even when all the papers were found to be correct, I still wouldn't say to you, 'Everything is arranged, now you are my child.'   No, I would wait until I knew that you really loved me a little, and then I would ask you some day, ' Would you like to become my child?'   Then if you answered, ' Yes, please, for I love you ', I would say, ' Then everything is settled. Here are the papers.   They were ready for a long time, but I was waiting until you, yourself, told me that you loved me and wanted to be my child.'

" Just so, the Lord Jesus arranged everything on the Cross a long time ago.   All that was necessary to make you a child of God was finished many centuries ago on Calvary when He died for your sins.   And now He asks you—and I may do it in His name—' Do you want to become a child of God?'

" If you say, ' Yes, please, Lord, for I love You ', then He'll say, ' Everything is settled now; I have been waiting a long time for that answer; now you are My child.'   Do you want to give the answer now to the Lord Jesus?"

Both of them spontaneously knelt down, and in their amusing Swiss–German language they said " Yes " to the Lord; and the angels in Heaven above rejoiced.

Their faces were radiant with happiness, and they were more beautiful than the mountains on the horizon. The sun had set, but the " Alpen-glow " changed the world into a bit of Heaven.   For some time the three of us continued to talk about the world of riches that the two little girls had now entered.

Children of God.

Once more I saw mountains before me in the sunset

glow. But now I was on the other side of the world. I was attending a meeting of students in the State of Washington on the west coast of the United States. We sat around a camp-fire and were having a " wiener roast ". We speared the Frankfurters on pointed sticks and roasted them in the fire.

The topic of our conversation was conversion. A boy asked, " How do you bring yourself to the point of conversion? Just what do you do to bring it about? You talk as if it were such an easy thing to do in order to become a child of God."

Was it the mountains in the distance that suddenly reminded me of the two little girls in Switzerland? I told the students about my experience, but one of them said, " I said ' yes ' to the Lord many years ago; what do you suppose is the reason that I've retrogressed so much since then? I sometimes doubt that I meant it seriously at the time."

A tall medical student answered him: " Once there was a boy who fell out of bed. His mother asked him how he happened to do that, and he answered, ' Mommy, it happened because I fell asleep too close to the place where I climbed in.' That is also what happens to many Christians. When they are converted they think that they have reached the goal. When one is converted, and says ' yes ' to Jesus, it does not mean the end of a new experience, but the beginning of it. It is as if one had entered a gate, the gate of conversion. To enter into the Kingdom of Heaven through the gate of conversion means to enter into a world of riches. All the promises in the Bible become your property. But you have to learn to find your way around in that world of riches. You have to find out what it means ' For all the promises of God in Him are yea, and in Him Amen ' (II Cor. 1 : 20). You have to find out how rich you are. If you think conversion means that you have arrived at the end of the pathway in your life, you will fall out, for then you fell asleep too close to the place where you climbed in."

Then I added, " At the moment of one's conversion he is registered in heaven as one who has earned all the rights and privileges that make one a multi-millionaire in a spiritual sense. Ephesians 1 : 3 : ' He who hath blessed us with all spiritual blessings in heavenly places in Christ.' "

The Bible is a cheque book. When you said " yes " to Jesus Christ, many promises were deposited to your credit at that very moment, and they were signed by the Lord Jesus Himself. But now you have to cash your cheques in order to profit by them. When you come upon such a promise and say, ' Thank you, Lord, I accept this ', then you have cashed a cheque, and that very day you'll be richer than you were the day before."

" Let's sing," a student suggested. The mountains re-echoed the hymn, " Every Day With Jesus is Better Than the Day Before ". One student remarked, " That's really true, at least if you cash no less than one cheque a day."

THE CHILDREN OF LIGHT MAY NOT
WALK IN DARKNESS

Firemen who straighten pictures in a burning house.

I WAS speaking at an American university on the subject of evangelism.

"If I straighten the pictures on the walls of your home, I am committing no sin, am I? But suppose that your house were afire, and I still went calmly about straightening pictures, what would you say? Would you think me merely stupid or very wicked? Why, you'd say I was not only stupid but wicked as well.

"The world today is on fire. What are you doing to extinguish the fire? Are you sitting in your study formulating theological concepts? Are you in training for a tennis tournament? These things are both good in themselves; but what are you doing to put out the fire? Your Communist brothers are busy forming cells. What are you doing?

"A Communist has written, 'The only people who can help the world in its present condition are the Christians; but they do not realize it.'

"Don't you understand? Has Jesus not said, 'You are the salt of the earth, the light of the world'?"

The children of light!

The next morning I was walking in the garden of the beautiful campus with a pretty co-ed. "Tell me," I said, " What are you doing to bring the Gospel to your fellow students?"

Her lovely face coloured as she said, " I feel very guilty this morning. I see myself suddenly as very much like the fireman who goes around straightening pictures while the house burns. I am a very self-conscious person. I have given my heart to Jesus, and I know that I am a child of God. But there is still a part of my shy retiring self living within an enclosure deep inside of me, and I become furious with anyone who approaches that enclosure. I have always felt that I had a right to live my own life. Recently I gave my testimony at our Club meeting, and they told me that my language and style and voice were quite good. So I know that I could speak in public. But if I should do so, people will see behind the enclosure, and that I will not have."

" Jeannie, it is only when we are crucified with Christ that we can enter into the joy of His resurrection. That sounds bad, but it is a loss that turns out to be a great gain. ' Whosoever shall lose his life for Christ's sake, shall save it.' Then you will find that His yoke is easy and His burden light. The time is short. To be lost for eternity is a dreadful thing, and to be used in saving others is such a wonderful experience."

People should see that we are ministers of Christ, to whom the stewardship of the mysteries of God has been entrusted. In the final analysis, the one requirement of such stewards is that they be " found faithful " (I Cor. 4:1–2).

In many places in the United States prayer meetings

are being held regularly for the specific purpose of praying for a revival. The privilege of speaking at these meetings with these people who are not merely grateful that they themselves are saved, but who also are full of love and compassion for a world lost in sin, always constitutes a high point in my life. I feel at home with people who see where the only solution really lies.

But there is another prerequisite for revival, besides that of prayer. For those who are seriously in earnest about this matter, there must be also a very personal and complete readiness to throw themselves wholeheartedly into the cause of the Gospel. Everything must be placed on the altar.

I once heard a sermon by the Reverend Oswald Smith at a conference in Switzerland. The following made a deep impression on me.

He held four books in his hands and asked, "Is everything on the altar? Have you lost your life for Christ's sake, your money, your time, your family, your home?"

He placed the four books on the table, "This is my money; this, my time; this, my family; this, my home. Yes, my money, all of it, except a small savings account which I have laid aside for my vacation.

"So, not all of my money." And he took one book from the table.

"My home, yes, except that I cannot take the children of my sister who is ill. They are so unruly that I just can't have them as guests in my home.

"So, not my home." And he removed the second book from the table.

" My time? Yes, it all belongs to the Lord. But my two weeks' vacation? I have a right to that, and have already reserved a room at the hotel.

" So, not my time." A third book disappeared.

" My family, yes, but I have not allowed my daughter to become what she so eagerly wishes to be, a missionary. We have a large family, and she must stay at home to help her mother.

"So, not my family." He picked up the fourth book.

The altar was empty.

I left the conference room and went out to walk alone, and I searched my heart. Was everything in my life on the altar? I was deeply touched. I understood very well what Oswald Smith meant. It was not a question of God's permitting His children to have their vacations. " Shall He not with Him also freely give us all things?"

" But seek ye first the kingdom of God, and His righteousness; and all these things shall be added unto you."

But in this losing for Christ's sake there may be no exceptions on our part. " Everything, Lord, except this one thing " will not do.

Can we rejoice in the resurrection life without having been crucified with Christ?

How much compromise there is!

I often wonder how it is possible that so many Christians live like beggars when we are Royal children, the very children of God. We appropriate one or two of His promises, but most of them we negate, or ignore, or —reject.

If indeed we have been "blessed with all spiritual blessings in heavenly places in Christ" (Eph. 1:3), why then do we still so often sigh? Are we really saved? Or is the devil right when he accuses us day and night? Is it true that we have been made "the righteousness of God in Christ"? (II Cor. 5:21).

Nietzsche has said, "Maybe I would have believed in a Redeemer if the Christians had looked more redeemed." Is it not written in Romans 5:5, "The love of God IS shed abroad in our hearts by the Holy Ghost which IS given unto us." Why, then, do people not see that love in our eyes? We so often live like carnal Christians.

Are we to be saved as by fire, and our works burned? (I Cor. 3:15).

This I do know, that we are living far below the level of what we actually are in Christ. How can this be? Is it perhaps that we do not really want to lose our lives for Christ's sake? If we want to save our lives we shall lose them.

May we then pray for a revival among others?

What about our churches in this respect? Does my church rejoice to learn that a revival has started in another church which is perhaps much more fundamental or more modernistic than ours? Will they be glad to hear that twenty people have been converted in that particular sect from whom they differ so much on the subject of chiliasm?

"That they all may be one, as Thou, Father, art in me, and I in Thee, that they also may be one in Us; that the world may believe that Thou hast sent Me " (John 17:21).

No?

How, then, can my church pray for a revival?

And what about my readiness to forgive the sins of others? Are the sins of my fellow-Christians in the depths of the sea? Is the reputation of all absent persons safe in my keeping? Or are their sins so firmly anchored ashore that if you should ask me anything about them I can tell you immediately all about their irritating or unlovely characteristics?

If this be true of me, may I then pray for a revival?

If I have so little understanding of the reality of God's promises that my problems seem greater than the victory of Christ, may I work toward a revival, even to the extent of praying for it?

Revive the world, O Lord, beginning with me!

Later on, I spoke to another group of students on the subject of revival, and mentioned among other things these high demands for those who wish to join in preparing for revival by praying for it.

" That means that I may not pray for a revival," said Lucy.

What? Was that to be the result? Had I made a mistake in establishing such lofty requirements? Should I be a little less positive about these things next time? Perhaps a bit of compromise might be more pedagogical?

That afternoon, Lucy and John took me with them in their car for a lovely trip through the mountains. It was a beautiful day. We picnicked in one of the state parks deep in the forest and later saw a magnificent sunset. The sky seemed to be suffused with the silhouettes of buildings and towers, which made it look like a fairy land of beautiful colours; gold, green, rose, and blue.

"Do you think heaven will look like that?" asked Lucy.

"When you stand at the gates of heaven you will have a bird's-eye view of your life," I replied. "I have often had to face death. It seems that then you see reality, you see the things in their proper perspective: the great things great, and the small things small."

"I think I shall see my sins as very large then," said Lucy.

"How do they look to you now?"

"Also very large. When you spoke about the lofty requirements we must fulfil before we may pray for a revival, I could see that I hadn't come nearly far enough to be equal to it."

"And do you just accept that situation?" asked John.

"Well, yes, I guess that's the way I am. I am a child of God, but certainly not a bit better than other Christians. After all, we are only human beings."

"From which direction do you suppose that remark came, from the Spirit of God or from the devil?" I said.

"I think, very likely, from the devil."

"And do you believe what he says? Don't you know that he is a liar from the beginning, and that he can do nothing but lie and deceive? If I always lied and boasted would you still listen to me? Of course you wouldn't. Why, then, do you listen to the devil?

"Do not forget that he is a conquered enemy. Jesus was sent to destroy the works of the devil. We do not have to take the responsibility for one single sin. 'If the Son therefore shall make you free, ye shall be free indeed' (John 8 : 36).

"Just think about what you said this morning: 'Then I may not pray for a revival.' Here is our world, so utterly bankrupt and unhappy that even the most indifferent person can see that we are headed for destruction. Not only are millions of people living without Christ, but they are facing an eternity without Him. We have seen in the course of history that revivals are used by God as a means of saving thousands of people for eternity. What you can do to help in this work is to pray for it with others. But you cannot do this as long as you hold on to your egotism, your selfishness, your pride, or whatever is your besetting sin.

"'All right then', you say; and you cling tightly to your ego and your sin, thinking that it is quite all right, and that life is even very pleasant that way. You don't see that you are bound, hand and foot, that you are losing your life by trying to save it.

"You do want to enjoy the resurrection life with Christ, but you refuse to be crucified with Him daily and to die unto self. The result is not only that you lead a poverty-stricken spiritual life, with little in it of the victory of Christ, but that this bleeding, perishing world is minus one more intercessor. Do awaken and see the reality of this truth. Give up your life for

Christ's sake, and you will save it.   Sanctification is not a burden, but a blessed release."

By now the sun had set, and darkness was closing in around us, although the sky was still suffused with gold. But before we started the homeward journey all three of us made a new commitment of ourselves to Him who prayed:

" As Thou hast sent Me into this world, even so have I also sent them into the world.   And for their sakes I sanctify Myself, that they also might be sanctified through the truth " (John 17: 18–19).

EVERLASTING LIFE

Nothing shall be able to separate me from the ocean of God's love, in Christ Jesus.

AS far astern as one could go on the deck of a freighter, I found a quiet spot where I could be delightfully alone.

I leaned on the rail and gazed at the silver wake left by our boat on the surface of the sea. Dolphins were leaping out of the water. Seven seagulls were circling around the ship. They would follow us faithfully until land was again within sight.

I mused.

What a tiny cockle-shell our vessel is on the immensity of the sea!

What a minute, insignificant, and temporal creature I am! Between my birth and my death I am permitted to live on this earth for some time and after that . . . eternity.

Where am I exactly?

Here I am aboard a tiny ship, and deep, deep under me is the sea, full of the mysterious life of marine animals. Above me is the infinite sky, out of which a tempest might come to wreck this little vessel. Around me is the endless sea, in which so many people have drowned.

Where, exactly, am I?

I live in a world where demons rule, where wars are

waged, where hopelessness, cruelty, and fear predomin-
ate, where millions of people are starving in China,
where cities are turned into ruins in many parts of
Europe; where atom bombs are surpassed in destructive
power by hydrogen bombs.

Exactly where am I?

I am in a world which God so loved, " that He gave
His only begotten Son, that whosoever believeth in
Him should not perish, but have everlasting life" (John
3 : 16).

I am on an earth where soon He shall come, even He
who has promised, " Behold, I make all things new "
(Rev. 21 : 5).

One day the earth, this beautiful earth, " shall be
filled with the knowledge of the glory of the Lord, as
the waters cover the sea " (Hab. 2 : 14).

Where am I exactly?

Already, at this moment, I am IN HIM.

And underneath me are His eternal arms.

This book was produced by the Christian Literature Crusade. We hope it has been helpful to you in living the Christian life. CLC is a literature mission with ministry in over 40 countries worldwide. If you would like to know more about us, or are interested in opportunities to serve with a faith mission, we invite you to write to:

Christian Literature Crusade
P.O. Box 1449
Fort Washington, PA 19034